# Raffia

# Raffia

## Claire E. Richards

The Art of Crafts

First published in 1998 by
The Crowood Press Ltd
Ramsbury, Marlborough
Wiltshire SN8 2HR

**British Library Cataloguing-in-Publication Data**

A catalogue record for this book is available from the British Library.

ISBN 1 86126 161 6

Typeface used: Melior

Photography by Philip Chambers
Designed and typeset by Focus Publishing, Sevenoaks, Kent
Printed and bound in China

# Contents

Acknowledgements . . . . . . . . . . . . . . . . . . . . . . 7

*Chapter*   1    Introduction . . . . . . . . . . . . . . 8

*Chapter*   2    Getting Started . . . . . . . . . . 11

*Chapter*   3    Dyeing Raffia . . . . . . . . . . . 13

*Chapter*   4    Plaiting . . . . . . . . . . . . . . . . 17

*Chapter*   5    Sewing . . . . . . . . . . . . . . . . . 27

*Chapter*   6    Starting a Hat . . . . . . . . . . . 33

*Chapter*   7    Hat Styles . . . . . . . . . . . . . . 43

*Chapter*   8    Bags . . . . . . . . . . . . . . . . . . 55

*Chapter*   9    Home Accessories . . . . . . . . 65

*Chapter*  10    Table Accessories . . . . . . . . 77

*Chapter*  11    Finishing Touches . . . . . . . . 83

*Chapter*  12    Child's Play . . . . . . . . . . . . . 91

Bibliography . . . . . . . . . . . . . . . . . . . . . . 92

Suppliers . . . . . . . . . . . . . . . . . . . . . . . . . 93

Index . . . . . . . . . . . . . . . . . . . . . . . . . . . . 95

# Acknowledgements

There is a great deal that a person can achieve individually, but there is much more that we can all achieve with love, help and support from those around us. I am very fortunate to have many important people around me. Thanks to Dad, Jane and Berni, Mick and Sue and Sara, Janet and John, Helena and John, Susie and Nic, Hilary and Robert, Jane H. and Sara H., all of whom have been encouraging for years, and certainly even more so lately. Thanks to Tom, Sam and Ben for donating valuable artwork – I'm sure you'll all be stars – and to George, for donating his photo.

Thanks also to all my students with whom I have learnt a great deal and had some really good times. There are too many classes to mention but some I particularly remember with a smile – Fittleworth, Carno, Gloucester and York, all in 1997, to name just a few, it was a vintage year. I have met some super women, which is a great bonus for any business.

Special thanks to Mum for the laughs, and for being a trusted co-pilot and assistant on many a country lane, with no petrol station in sight.

To Lynn, my love and thanks for your support and continued friendship. And never forgetting Pete, who has been there from the start, giving unending support and putting up with considerable mess, dubious prototypes and glue-gun traumas. Thanks, my love.

# 1 Introduction

## ORIGINS

Raffia is the leaf of the Raphia species of palm tree indigenous to tropical forests. The type most widely used for craft work (and for tidying gardens) comes from the Raphia ruffia tree of Madagascar. All Raphia palms have a short stem, or no stem at all. Their gigantic feather leaves are typically 9–15 metres long, and sometimes as much as 20 metres, making them some of the biggest leaves of the plant kingdom.

To get the raffia, the leaves are removed whole and the stem of the leaf is stripped to leave the raffia 'thread'. Although the younger leaves are used, they are already approximately 1.5–2 metres in length.

Within its native Africa, raffia (or raphia) has for a long time been an important part of life and of the economy, providing a material for ropes, fishing tackle and snares. In addition, the pulp can make an effective fish poison, the tree can be tapped to produce palm wine, and roofing poles, stools, and loom beams have been built from the palm. Rotting palm logs are also the source of a large white maggot considered by certain tribes to be a delicacy – dead or alive.

Although imports of various commodities, including cotton cloth and packaging material, have affected the craft, the weaving of raphia cloth has been for many years a tradition in several parts of Africa. As in the craft work practised today, this would also involve dyeing of the raphia. The fine thread would be woven, using various styles of loom, to produce brightly coloured skirts, wraps and bags. The continuous thread needed for the weaving would be prepared by young children of the tribe, who would patiently knot the lengths of raffia. Traditionally, raphia weaving was a male craft in Africa, and boys would start to receive training as early as six years old from a master weaver in the tribe. The training period would be about six months.

Although traditional African crafts were still enjoying government support and success as recently as the 1970s, when an exhibition at a trade fair promoted the making of raffia hats, tea cosies, slippers and table mats, there was also evidence that the work being produced was not of as high a quality as it had been in the past. Increasing commercialism and higher-education opportunities have led to more and more Africans moving away from traditional crafts.

## A COTTAGE INDUSTRY

In the UK, the principle of plaiting being used to create hats is certainly not a new one. From the end of the seventeenth century to the 1870s, Hertfordshire and Bedfordshire enjoyed a lucrative time as producers of straw plaiting; Luton became the centre of the country's hat industry. Hats and bonnets were made of straw, which needed to be plaited by hand before it could be used, and it was not unusual for a mother and her children to earn twice as much in a week as the man of the household.

The straw plaiting of the eighteenth and nineteenth centuries was a much harder version of the raffia method described in this book. The plait produced was often as narrow as a quarter of an inch, and the straw was usually only ten inches in length and needed to be kept moist and supple.

The straw-plaiting industry used child labour. Taught by parents from the age of three, poor children were sent to plaiting schools, particularly in the villages around Luton; there, they were given a rudimentary education, but they attended primarily in order to learn about plaiting. While some schools did offer a sound education, others really only represented a form of organized child labour. At one time, there were 13,000 children going to these schools.

The decline in this industry in the late nineteenth century was due to a number of factors: the introduction of compulsory education in the 1870s, which also banned straw plaiting in schools; the introduction of the manufacture of felt hats; and the commercial efforts of the Japanese, who exported good-quality plait to the UK at 3d a score, at a time when it cost 10d a score to produce in the UK.

It did not take long, however, for raffia to work its way back into schools, this time in a more positive way. It was no longer a form of child labour, but, as Annie Wadsworth wrote in *Practical Raffia-Work – An Exemplification of the Use of Raffia with Shapes and Skeleton Frames, and in Embroidery*, a means for children to be stimulated and to learn to 'reason and construct by means of handwork'. Written in the early twentieth century, *Practical Raffia-Work* did not include any plaiting techniques; its projects concentrated on twisting raffia around cut shapes or embroidery on raffia-canvas or stitching-canvas. The children could create many and varied items, including hair-tidies, collar- and glove-boxes, toilet-tidies, serviette rings, table mats and plant-pot covers. Some of these re-appear in this book, although considerably up-dated!

A sales list at the back of *Practical Raffia-Work* includes a raffia-weaving loom similar to those used traditionally in Africa, while a price list shows Natural Raffia in 1lb bundles at a shilling per lb. How I wish some things had not changed.

It is not certain when this craft work stopped in schools, although many people now in their sixties and seventies talk to me at shows about working with raffia in school. They have clear memories of making table mats and other useful items.

The recent growth of interest in raffia work in the UK can probably be more easily explained. It is unrelated to schooling – it seems from my conversations that the craft stopped in schools with the introduction of new craft work and a new curriculum. The clear link for most people in the UK who now create raffia hats is, in fact, Australia. It is difficult to say how the craft took a hold in Australia, but it was probably because of the enormous and vital demand for attractive, durable and sun-proof hats. Without doubt, hat-making has remained the most popular part of the craft.

The craft is particularly flexible and user-friendly. I have taught over 400 people, and have sold several hundred hats, but I am still delighted by how differently all the hats have turned out and how students make them so individual by the trims and decorations.

Like all crafts, raffia work should be as free of stress and as enjoyable as possible. I hope you find the instructions and diagrams easy to follow, and therefore key in keeping your stress levels down.

# 2 Getting Started

## MATERIALS

Probably the most important part of working with raffia is to ensure you use the best quality of material available. Raffia is now a popular material for use in flower arrangements or gardening, but it is still not readily available in the quantity or quality that is needed for plaiting a hat or bag. For details of suppliers of good-quality raffia, see page 93.

Once you have purchased your raffia, you need to weigh out as much as you need for a particular project. I use a supermarket carrier bag balanced on top of my kitchen scales. If you plan to colour the raffia, you need to make sure that you weigh out more than enough – I call this my 'dye margin' – to make sure that you have enough to plait, sew (which can take a surprising amount) and decorate your item. As an example, an average hat will need approximately 300 grams; if the raffia is to be dyed, measure out 400 grams. It is very likely you will have some left over at the end of the project, but you should not find yourself short and unable to finish the project. If

you have experimented with a different colour, or used natural dyes, it may be extremely difficult to reproduce exactly the effect if you do run out.

## SORTING

As raffia is a leaf, you will always see natural variations in your material. All raffia workers need to be careful about these variations, and they probably represent one of the main difficulties of the craft.

## Note:

For the majority of the items in the book, you need to work with a five-thread knot; check the item you want to make before you continue.

## Choosing Threads

Sift through the raffia and pull out five (or fewer) good-quality threads. It is difficult to be precise about what constitutes a good-quality thread, as one of the main advantages of the craft is that it is approximate – there is very little that needs to be exact.

Generally, you should be looking for threads of raffia that are not too thin, but do not look too fat either. You may find, for example, that your particular bundle of raffia is extremely fat; in that case, you would not want to use five threads, as the result would be very chunky. You might consider only four or even just three threads.

**USEFUL TIP:**
You may want to colour the raffia after this weighing stage. You will see from the chapter on dyeing that I sort the raffia before I colour, as I find it easier to manage, and it also means that I am not dyeing 'rubbish'. The choice is yours.

Opposite: The basic equipment for getting started.

You also do not need to worry if the threads are of different lengths. Generally, you will find that there is a clean-cut end and a messy end. Put the clean ends together. Collect the five (or fewer) threads and tie a knot close to the cut end.

## Rubbish

As you continue sorting through the raffia, you will probably come across 'rubbish', including raffia that is twig-like, maybe very stiff, green or sharp (you might get the occasional splinter). I recommend that you do not use this – it will be difficult to work with and will provide a glaring contrast to the rest of your item. (If you are making a hat, it is a sure bet that it will end up in pride of place right at the front!) You also tend to find that the rubbish breaks easily, whereas good-quality raffia is harder to 'snap'. Do not worry if you do not catch every piece of rubbish as you sort, as you will have plenty of opportunities to discard these pieces later.

## Note:

If you have already dyed your raffia, you will find that the 'rubbish' is easier to identify, as it does not tend to take the colour as well as the rest of the raffia.

You will also find small clumps of 'wispy' raffia, and I do not recommend that you use these. At this stage, you may start to become concerned about the waste, but don't worry. Many of the projects take a considerable amount of time (approximately 8–10 hours for a hat), so you do not want to use raffia that is not at its best. You may find that a pet gerbil or hamster finds the wispy raffia quite acceptable for a den.

Sorting out the rubbish is usually the most tedious part of the whole process, so I usually go through the complete bundle and get rid of it all at the beginning. However, whatever you are making, do not knot all the raffia. If you aim for approximately three-quarters of the total amount, this will ensure that you have threads available for sewing and decorating if you need them. This way, you will not need to unravel the plait in order to have sewing raffia, and if you do need to plait more it is easy to add on to the end.

## Dyeing

If you have not already coloured the raffia before sorting, now is definitely the time to do so. Once you start plaiting, the raffia becomes too dense to dye successfully. You might be able to get the colour into the item, but you would probably not be able to get it all out, and it would be very difficult to get the finished item completely dry.

# 3 Dyeing Raffia

## THE PLEASURES OF DYEING

Playing around with different colours is probably one of the most enjoyable features of working with raffia. I have found it an easy material to colour and, as it does not all completely dye, it maintains a very natural and unique 'flecked' look, which adds to the appeal. I derive great satisfaction from making a complementary hat to go with a particular outfit, when it is possible to strike lucky with the dye and get the colour spot on. However, as the range of any one colour is so wide, I usually promise to complement, rather than commit to an exact match.

In the case of home accessories, being able to colour the raffia means that you can make items for your home, or gifts for friends, that fit in with a particular décor. It is a satisfying result, and saves hours scouring the shops trying to match colours.

## THE PROCESS

The process of dyeing raffia is not complicated – the most important and most time-consuming part is rinsing the excess dye out of the raffia. This is particularly crucial for a hat, and you ignore this warning at your own peril! I do not use any pre-dye solutions, salt or fixers, for any of the methods listed. In my view, the items, particularly hats, gain character with wear, and with the effect of the sun year on year.

I use dyes from the synthetic Dylon range, but if you are familiar with the techniques you can obviously use natural dyes just as easily. I stick to the synthetic dyes because they are so readily available. Also, if I want to repeat a colour, I have more chance of getting close to it with the synthetic dyes.

It is important to note here that two people following exactly the same dyeing process, using the same colour, might still produce different end results with slight variations. This could be due to varying water temperatures, variations in the raffia – one leaf is not always exactly the same colour as another – or in the amount of time that the raffia is left in the dye solution.

A few dyed items.

Dyeing raffia is subject to the usual colour rules – blue on yellow will result in green, and so on. Unfortunately, this means that for those colours that need white to start with, it is impossible, as the raffia cannot be white enough before you start. This is another part of the craft with which I enjoy experimenting (unless I am under pressure to find a particular colour for a customer).

The following methods are all ones that I have used. Choose the method that suits you, according to the available time and space, and depending on what you are planning to make. I also find it much easier to dye and dry the raffia (particularly larger amounts) if it is already knotted and bundled.

## Note:

If you want to produce black raffia, you must use the Boiled Method.

The basic dyeing equipment.

# DYEING METHODS

## Hot Water Method

This is the method that I use the most for my hats, as it gives a good depth of colour in return for minimum fuss, and I can easily double up the amounts (raffia and dye) to increase my stock of different shades.

*EQUIPMENT*

- plastic 'muck bucket' or container large enough for the amount of raffia
- 1 Dylon Multi-Purpose Dye
- pair of rubber gloves
- large wooden spoon (or similar)
- approximately 400g (14oz) raffia (maximum) for one Dylon Multi-Purpose Dye

*INSTRUCTIONS*

1.  Fill the container with hot water from the tap. Use the spoon (or similar) to stir in the dye once you have sufficient water.

2.  Place the raffia in the solution and pour in more hot water, until the raffia is fully submerged.

3.  Continue to stir for about 10 minutes, making sure that all the raffia is in contact with the dye solution.

4.  Leave the raffia to sit in the dye for about one hour, returning to stir every so often.

5.  Start to empty the water from the container, leaving the raffia in place.

6. Rinse thoroughly with cold water, repeating the process until the water runs clear. You may only need to rinse the raffia twice, but you may need to do it up to six times – there are no set rules.

7. To dry the raffia, you can either simply throw it on the lawn, on a sheet, or hang it over the washing line. If the weather is not good, you can hang it over the bath, either on a line or on a drying frame, or rig up a line in the garage. It is best to let the raffia dry naturally, so do not feel tempted to put it in the tumble dryer.

## Boiled Method

I use this method if I want a very rich version of a colour. The difference in results between the hot water method and this choice are quite dramatic, and both have their own appeal. It is worth noting that neither seems to fade more than the other. However, the boiled method produces a much deeper colour to start with, which means that it will always be that much darker.

I would not recommend using a pot that you might want to use for cooking again, as the dye 'bleeds' into the pot. I have used the same pot for different colours and the dye on the pot does not seem to come out into the next colour, but I would not guarantee this for jam!

*EQUIPMENT*

- metal container large enough for the amount of raffia
- 1 Dylon Multi-Purpose Dye
- large wooden spoon (or similar)
- approximately 400g (14oz) raffia (maximum) for one Dylon Multi-Purpose Dye

*INSTRUCTIONS*

1. Half-fill your container with hot water, either from the tap or the kettle. Dissolve the dye to be used.

2. Pour in further hot water, enough to cover the amount of raffia you will be colouring. Do not put the raffia in yet.

3. Put the container on the stove and bring to the boil. You will need to keep an eye on it, to make sure that it does not bubble too much and cover your cooker top with colour.

4. Remove from the heat to safeguard against the raffia catching fire.

5. Gently place the raffia into the dye solution, and return the pan to the heat.

6. Gently simmer for about half an hour, making sure you keep the raffia submerged; it can rise out of the pan and will not be properly coloured.

7. After the necessary time, remove from the heat, rinse the raffia thoroughly with cold water and dry it as for the Hot Water Method.

**USEFUL TIP:**
You might find it useful to colour two loads of raffia with the same dyewater, but note that the second load of raffia will be lighter in colour than the first.

## (Automatic) Washing Machine Method

This is the easiest method of dyeing raffia, but, because of the amount of water it uses, it is probably not worth doing small amounts in this way. This method is ideal if you want to colour enough raffia for two large items, particularly if you would like them to match. Although some manufacturers' instructions recommend using machine dye, I have had good results using the multi-purpose range. The method for both is the same.

Dyed raffia pots: attractive and practical.

*EQUIPMENT*

◆ pillowcase or washing bag large enough to take the amount of raffia
◆ 1 Dylon Multi-Purpose Dye for approximately 400g (14oz) dried raffia

*INSTRUCTIONS*

1.  Dissolve the dye in half a litre (about a pint) of boiling water and pour the solution into the drum of the washing machine.

2.  Place raffia in zipped washing bags or pillowcases that you do not mind colouring. It is important to secure the top of the bag or pillowcase, otherwise the raffia will become tangled in the machine and will probably clog your pipes.

3.  Dampen the raffia in the bags and place them inside the washing machine.

4.  Use the longest, hottest wash available on your machine (without pre-wash), and let the machine run through the complete wash and rinse cycle.

5.  Do not allow the raffia to be spun for the full amount of time, but stop the machine after a short spin. This prevents the raffia from getting too battered through the full spin, and becoming 'shredded'.

6.  Remove the raffia, and dry it according to previous methods.

7.  Finally, rinse your washing machine by running the longest hottest cycle again, this time with a small amount of washing powder (do not put too much in, otherwise you might find your kitchen overcome by suds), and one cup of bleach.

# 4 Plaiting

## PLAITING SKILLS

The plaiting and sewing are the 'backbone' of all raffia projects. In making some of the items in this book, you may spend three to eight hours plaiting, so plaiting skills are crucial to the look of the finished object.

Most people have already done some plaiting, usually using three strands and working as tightly as possible, in order to secure what they are doing. With raffia, it is not necessary to be so concerned with tension, or ensuring that the plait is secure. In undertaking three to eight hours of plaiting, you need to work in as relaxed a manner, and environment, as possible. I have noticed that the more my students transfer any stress they feel to their plait, making it very tight, the more tight and 'stressed' their projects turn out. Your aim should be to strike a happy medium between too tight, or stressed, and too loose, or relaxed. Most students develop this very quickly.

## ADDING OTHER MATERIALS

You might choose to include other materials in with your raffia plait, either to create a special effect, or to add a little strength to the final product. I have experimented with seagrass, leather, wool and silky cotton, and all have worked well.

Examples of five-thread, four-knot plaits, from top to bottom: the ideal width; too loose; too tight.

Items plaited with raffia and 'alien' materials.

Opposite: Using more than one colour. Table mat shapes showing (left to right) the blend method and the block method.

was a great success. It had the general look of a raffia bag, but with added strength from the seagrass.

## Leather
I incorporated the leather bootlaces with increased strength in mind, using them to help make the handles on my bucket bag that bit stronger. The result was the strength I was after and also a comfortable feel to the handles.

## Wool
For the brown sun hat, I tried a chocolate-coloured chenille, which gave an interesting 'chocolate chip' effect.

## Silky Cotton
For the raffia box, I used a silk-type cotton. My aim with this, and with the chenille, was to get a different finish, and this was easily achieved.

# TWO OR MORE COLOURS

If you do not want to work with only one colour, you can mix colours to interesting effect. For hats, this is particularly useful where you have an outfit that is a mixture of colour, or where you want to produce a functional hat that can be used with many outfits. For other raffia projects, the principle is

The method for using each type of material was exactly the same. Using the four plait, five threads to a knot method, choose one strand and add the extra material to it. Do not plait with the extra material as one of the four strands, but incorporate it within a strand, this avoids the plait becoming too uneven, where the extra material might 'pull' too much on the other raffia strands.

(For each of the items shown, I have only incorporated one piece of extra material into one of the strands. If you want the extra material to be even more evident, simply include it into more than one strand.)

## Seagrass
I used this in the small attaché bag, as I am always concerned with trying to make the bags stronger, without detracting from the raffia look. Although it felt a little bulky to work with, and sewing was slower (because of having to avoid the seagrass), the final product

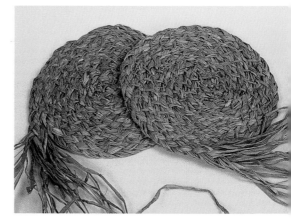

exactly the same, and you can have fun creating more individual items. Some of my more interesting pieces – for example, bags – have been made up using a medley of colours.

There are two ways to use more than one colour at a time. You can produce the plait using the 'blend' effect or the 'block' effect.

## Blend Method

The example illustrated uses two deliberately contrasting colours, but generally the effect of the blend method is soft, with the colours not quite so evident. I have demonstrated using two colours, but there is scope to use up to twenty colours for this method, which means it is ideal if you have left-over bundles of raffia and want to make an interesting, and completely unique, item.

*INSTRUCTIONS*

1.   Prepare the knots for plaiting, using a mixture of colour in each knot – one knot may have three strands of colour A and two strands of colour B, while another many have two As and three Bs. Obviously, if you use more of one colour than another, the emphasis of colour in the item will be different.

2.   Start the plait with knots and strands jumbled as you like; there is no need to keep the colours segregated. Add the blended knots as normal, as you continue plaiting.

3.   Trim as normal and sew with whichever colour you prefer.

## Note:
The choice of sewing colour for this method is even less important than with

the Block Method, as it will simply add to the mixture of colour throughout the item.

## Block Method

The illustration showing this method deliberately uses the same colours as used for the blend method, so the contrast between the methods can be easily compared. This method is named after the final effect produced, where each shade is prominent in 'blocks' of colour. The method described below uses two colours, although you can use up to four in the same way:

1.   Take two knots of colour A, and two of colour B.

2.   Start the plait with colours in the order A, B, A, B, making sure when you plait that you do not 'mix' the strands at all, and that you only add a colour A knot to an A strand, and a B knot to a B strand.

3.   Continue the plait and trim as normal, and sew with whichever colour you prefer.

## Note:
The raffia used for sewing has very little impact on which is the more visible colour, as the big pieces of colour characteristic of the block effect are the most striking feature of this method.

## STARTING PLAITING

For the projects in this book I recommend a four plait, done with much less tension than you would need if you were trying to plait hair or a horse tail, and make it stay neat. A three plait

(Left to right) the blend and block methods over a larger area.

tends to provide a plait that is too tubular, and will add extra bulk (and weight) to the item, giving a cumbersome finish.

Some people work with a five plait. You are really only limited in the size of your plait by your ability to control the raffia while you are working. A twelve plait is certainly not impossible, although this is the widest I have ever worked to.

## FOUR-KNOT PLAIT

*EQUIPMENT*

◆ good supply of raffia knots
◆ bulldog clip or pegs
◆ something to tie on to

*INSTRUCTIONS*

## Note:
If you are left-handed, follow the instructions in parentheses. If you are right-handed you will get used to doing everything on the right, while left-handed people will do everything starting on the left.

1.    Pick four of the knots you have tied and secure them while you work with a bulldog clip or pegs over the back of a chair, tied on to a door handle or knob, a banister, a child's pushchair, an ironing board.

Opposite: Keeping the plait still, using the back of a chair.

2.    This securing in place is important. While you do not want to pull the plait tight, you need it to be still while you are plaiting. You cannot create the right mixture of tension and flexibility in the plait with the raffia unsecured. Do not worry if your, for example, chair, is such that you have to tie on a considerable amount of the knots, and you are only left with a short amount of raffia to work with before you get to the scruffy ends. Once you get under way with the plaiting, you will be able to turn the plait around and complete the raffia you have secured to the chair, so that this is not wasted.

3.    Divide the four knots into approximately equal-sized 'free-flowing' strands. These strands do not have to be the same divisions as the original knots, but it is very important that they form four free-flowing separate pieces at all times. If the strands become tangled, it will be very difficult, maybe impossible, to correct.

Working from the right, and holding the 1st strand, move this over the 2nd, under the 3rd and over the 4th, and pull it through to the left-hand side.

Fig 1: Right-hand plaiting

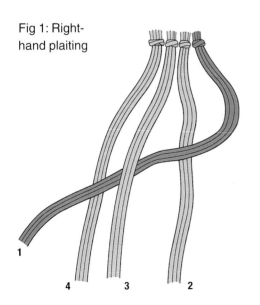

(Working from the left, and holding the 1st strand, move this over the 2nd, under the 3rd and over the 4th, and pull it through to the right-hand side.)

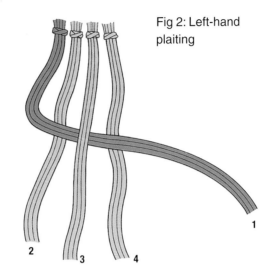

Fig 2: Left-hand plaiting

Make sure when you work that you are not pulling the raffia too tensely and creating too tight a plait. This will create too dense an item, while a too loose plait will create an item which will have too many gaps. The ideal is to have something that is flexible but not loose (see photo page 17).

It is also worth remembering that a hat, for example, needs about 11m of plait. If you create too tight a plait, it will take you considerably longer to make.

The angle you are aiming to replicate, when working across the plait is not a tight 90 degrees, but much nearer to 45 degrees.

4.    Once you have got the first strand through to the left (right), you start over again with the strand that is now on the extreme right (left). This becomes your next 1st strand and you keep repeating the process – over the 2nd, under the 3rd and over the 4th, then pull it through. The process of 'pulling

through' helps the strands remain free flowing and ensures that they do not get tangled.

5. Every so often, you need to flatten the plait between finger and thumb. This helps to ensure you have a flat, rather than a tubular plait.

6. As the plait gets longer, do not try to work too close to your body. Instead, remove the peg or bulldog clip, move the plait further along your secure point, and re-secure. Plaiting too close to your body becomes difficult and you will not be able to maintain a firm hold on the plait if you allow it to hang limply.

## Adding New Knots – Keeping the Plait Alive

Continue plaiting as described until one of your strands starts to become 'weak' – short or thin. Avoid letting the strand become too weak – try to maintain approximately 25cm (10in) before the complete end of a strand. As each item is one continuous plait, you need to learn how to keep the plait 'alive'. At the beginning of a plait this can be quite tricky to judge. You need to avoid letting your strands become too weak together. However, as the raffia is generally of a similar length from a bundle, and you have started the strands together, it is quite likely that they will get weak and die together.

In order to 'stagger in' new knots, you may need to decide to 'sacrifice' a strand when you do not consider it to be too weak. If you do not stagger in the new knots, you will add too much weight to your plait in too short a space, and the result will be very bulky.

1. Put the weak strand in the 1st position (right for right-handed, left for left-handed), and take it over the 2nd strand as normal.

2. Take a fresh knot, lay it on top of the weak strand, with the knot protruding upwards on the right (left) and continue plaiting with both the weak and the new – under the 3rd, over the 4th, and pull through.

3. When you add a new knot, do not try to secure it into the plait with the knot too close to the plait; you will find it easier to have perhaps 4cm (1in) of the new knot hanging off the edge of the plait, especially as you will need to cut this knot off later. At first, the plait will feel and look fatter, but do not worry.

By blending in new knots in this way you will ensure that dying strands are secured in place with new ones. This means that, by the time the plait is sewn into shape, it will be practically impossible for it to unwind. It is not unusual to plait with parts of an old and new strand together for maybe 12cm

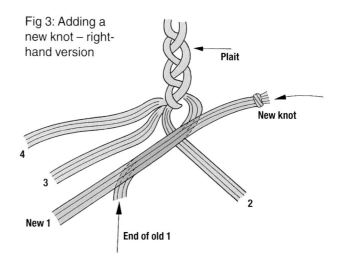

Fig 3: Adding a new knot – right-hand version

Plait

New knot

4

3

New 1

End of old 1

2

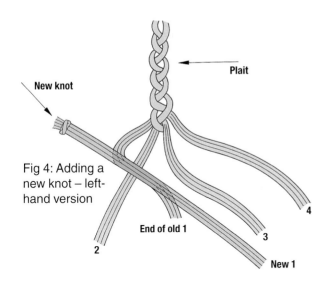

**New knot**

**Plait**

**Fig 4: Adding a new knot – left-hand version**

**End of old 1**

**2**

**New 1**

**3**

**4**

brittle, twiggy and wispy. Get into the habit of dropping these bits out of the plait, to be trimmed off later. As you stagger the introduction of the new strands, and gradually drop the old bits, the bulkiness will even out, and the dropping will help to improve the finished product.

Continue plaiting and adding to weak strands until you have used all your prepared knots. You should still have raffia available for sewing and decorating.

(5in), which makes the plait very secure.

Continue plaiting until you need to add another knot to the next weak strand. Repeat the adding process, always making sure that the weak strand is in the 1st position (on the right or left). Ideally, stagger the introduction of each new knot to reduce the immediate impact of too much extra weight in a small area of plait. The ideal minimum distance to aim for between each new knot is approximately 8cm (3in).

Once you have staggered in new knots to each strand for the first time, the theory is that the strands will start to 'stagger out' naturally. However, as there can be no guarantee of a consistent length in the raffia, this does not always happen as planned, so you will need to keep a keen eye on the 'health' of all strands.

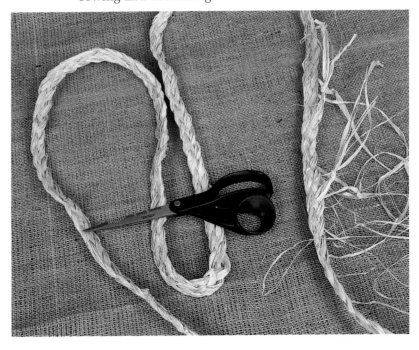

## Discarding Rubbish

At the same time as you start adding new knots, you need to discard any rubbish that you discover. This will be particularly necessary as you are working towards the scruffy ends of the strands, where it is likely to be getting

## Trimming

Before you can start sewing, you will need to trim your plait thoroughly. This is very easy to do.

You can cut flush to the plait the rubbish that you left hanging out of the plait. The knots that you have added

A length of plait showing a trimmed section and untrimmed, with rubbish and new knots hanging.

you will not want to cut as close to the plait. It is better to cut these in line with the edge of the plait; when you start to shape your item, this will help stop any ends popping out.

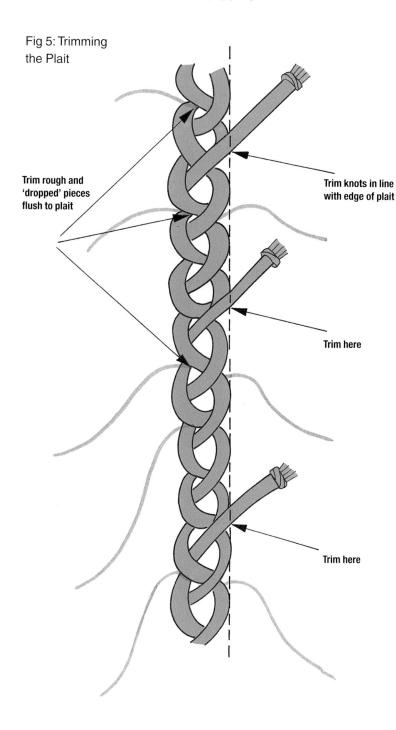

Fig 5: Trimming the Plait

**Trim rough and 'dropped' pieces flush to plait**

**Trim knots in line with edge of plait**

**Trim here**

**Trim here**

## Creating the Bushy Tail

For all the raffia items it is important to have a bushy tail. This is a landmark to help you know where to start a different part of the item, change direction or finish. The procedure for creating the bushy tail is the same for all items.

1.    Once you have trimmed your plait, take a long piece of healthy raffia thread (always use good-quality raffia for this), and place it around the top of your plait near where the pattern of the plait starts. With the trimmed side – the side on which you added your new knots – facing upwards, tie a secure reef knot.

2.    Approximately 2cm (1in) from the knot you have just tied, cut off the beginning (the first four knots, the unplaited section) of the plait. Be careful not to cut the long strand you have just tied on, as you will use this to start sewing. This will leave you with a 'bushy tail'.

3.    Once you have plaited, trimmed and created your bushy tail you are ready to start sewing your item. Refer to the sewing section and the instructions for each particular item.

## PLAITING CHECKLIST

1.    Raffia threads make a knot. Plaiting involves four strands made up of old and new knots.

2.    It is not necessary to be too concerned with tension or with trying to ensure that the plait is 'secure'.

3.    Try not to make your plaiting too 'stressed'; it is more likely to feel very bulky and dense.

4.   Find the ideal distance away from whatever you secure your plait to while working, and keep moving the bulldog clip or peg along the plait to this distance. This stops the plait getting too lax, and losing all tension.

5.   Keep each of the strands free flowing; it is essential that they do not become tangled together.

6.   Always remember to pull the first strand through when you get to the extreme left (right) – in effect, when it has become the 4th strand.

7.   Make sure the 1st strand is free flowing before you start working it across.

8.   Do not work across the plait at too tight an angle, but work 'downwards' to help make the plait grow.

9.   Remember to flatten the plait every so often to stop it getting too tubular.

10.   Consider 'sacrificing' a healthy strand when you first start plaiting. This will help you 'stagger in' new knots later, and avoid a bulky look to the plait.

11.   Do not let strands become too weak before adding a new knot – you want the old strand and new knot to work together, as this keeps them secure.

12.   Discard any rubbish as you like. This helps to keep the plait even in width and look. Do not worry about discarding healthy threads – you are interested in a nice-looking plait.

13.   Trim the rubbish close to the plait. Do not trim the added knots as close to the plait, but trim in line with the outside edge of the width.

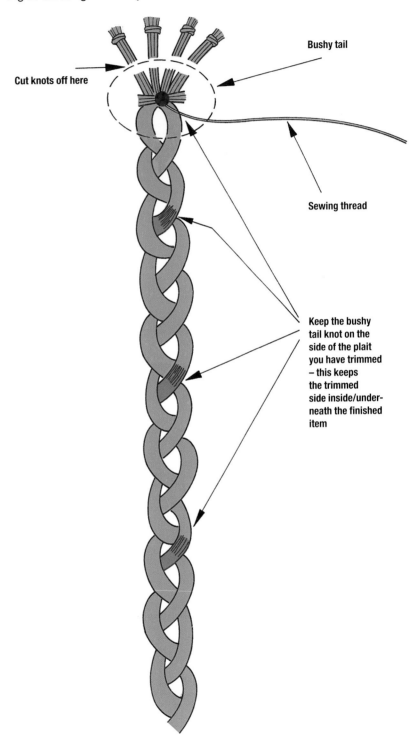

Fig 6: Creating the bushy tail

Cut knots off here

Bushy tail

Sewing thread

Keep the bushy tail knot on the side of the plait you have trimmed – this keeps the trimmed side inside/underneath the finished item

# 5 Sewing

While I have been teaching raffia classes, I have met students with many different levels of sewing ability, from those who are beautiful embroiderers to those who have never sewn on so much as a button. With almost no exceptions, I have found that those with more sewing experience are actually disadvantaged in sewing raffia (although those who cannot manage it successfully are still very few and far between). In the case of nearly all the projects in the book, big is definitely beautiful when it comes to sewing, so do not be put off if your sewing skills are rusty or are newly learnt. A favourite maxim of mine is that you do not have to be either a beautiful knotter, a beautiful plaiter or a beautiful sewer to be able to make beautiful raffia work.

## SEWING BASICS

The principles for sewing vary little from item to item. However, before you can start sewing, you must refer to the instructions for the particular item you want to make. The 'first turn' with the bushy tail is very important in determining the shape of the item.

**USEFUL TIP:**
Before you thread your needle, ensure that the knot at the start of the plait is on the trimmed side. This will mean that any rough ends are kept on the inside or underneath of the item.

Along with the plaiting, this is really the mainstay of the craft, so it might be worthwhile to review the Sewing Checklist (see page 31) before you begin sewing (and during, if you are struggling a little).

*EQUIPMENT*

- plait of required length and width for the particular item
- needle
- raffia for sewing (must be healthy and long)
- mould for particular item
- sellotape (to secure to mould)

**Note:**
The style of needle you use really depends on personal preference. I have used different needles for different jobs; sometimes a curved one is better, and at other times I prefer a straight needle. Either way, try a selection. However, more important than shape is the need

Below: The basic equipment needed: the plait, raffia for sewing, a needle, scissors, a mould and sellotape.

Opposite: A bucket bag and a Breton hat showing more than one colour, incorporated using the dead end method.

for a sharp and sturdy needle, and a large eye to take the thicker raffia.

*INSTRUCTIONS*

## Note:

Left-handed people should follow the instructions in parentheses where they appear.

1. Thread your needle on the long piece of raffia that is attached near your bushy tail – see Creating the Bushy Tail (page 24).

2. Refer to the particular item instructions before continuing.

> **USEFUL TIP:**
> If the end of your raffia is a little lumpy, it might be easier to thread if your raffia is folded.

3. Once you know how big and what shape your first turn must be, start sewing by turning the bushy tail to the right (left) for the required distance and tucking under the opposite plait.

4. Stitch from the bushy tail side (the inside/underneath of the object) through to the outside, through both pieces of plait.

> **USEFUL TIP:**
> It is usual for the first turn to create a gap; you should not force the plait to sit edge to edge. The purpose of the sewing will be to close down the gaps between the edges.

Right: Example of a first turn with the bushy tail. This is the right-hand version and the oval turn is suitable for the start of a hat. A different item may need a different first turn. Note the first stitch comes through both piece of plait. See also the gap created by the first turn.

Far right: The first stitches (the right-hand version).

> **USEFUL TIP:**
> Always sew through the plait and not through the gaps in the plait, otherwise you will simply make the gaps bigger.

## Note:

Never pull your stitches really tight; with your sewing you are aiming to bring the plait edges gently together. If you pull the stitches too tight, it will buckle the item, and this may be very difficult to correct.

5. Close the gap by sewing up through the left (right) plait and down through the right (left) plait, working simply to close down any gaps.

## Note:

You are only concerned with the part of the plait you are sewing; do not worry if the outside edges of the plait start to gape.

6. After closing the gap, on the inside/underneath, feed your needle through the plait back to the bushy tail. It does not matter how you get the needle back to the tail; it is not necessary to sew through the plait to the outside of the item.

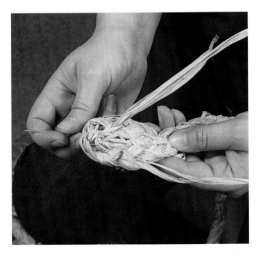

also that you do not overlap the plait while you are sewing – the aim is simply to keep the plait edge to edge. Where you encounter gaps that may be created when sewing the previous row, simply pull your stitches a fraction tighter to close down the gaps.

8. To thread new raffia, pull your needle off on the inside/underneath of your project (bushy tail side). Thread a new piece and push the needle through from the tail side to the outside, directly next to where your old end is hanging. Tie a double knot with both the old and new ends when they get level.

9. Trim the knot, not too close to the plait. (Depending on the item you are

Left: Closing down the first gap (the right-hand version); note the 'lumps' and 'gaps' at the top of the turn – do not worry about this.

## Note:
It is important to return the sewing thread to the bushy tail at this time. If

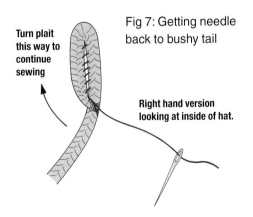

Turn plait this way to continue sewing

Fig 7: Getting needle back to bushy tail

Right hand version looking at inside of hat.

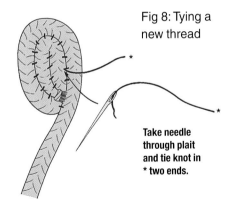

Fig 8: Tying a new thread

Take needle through plait and tie knot in * two ends.

you do not, you will see that you are in the wrong position to continue sewing the plait.

7. Turn the plait over so you cannot see the bushy tail – looking at the outside/top of the item. Gently turn the unsewn plait to the left (right) and continue sewing the shape to the required size.

## Note:
Make sure you keep your stitches comfortable, and not too tight. Ensure

making, the ends may become slightly frayed.)

## Note:
When you have tied on a new thread, your sewing will be 'out of sequence' with your previous pattern, that is, the needle will be positioned to come up the wrong part of the item. Always sew towards yourself and up the joining piece of plait, and down the already sewn section. To get back into sequence, simply take the newly threaded needle back through the item (without making a

new stitch), and return to the previous pattern.

10. Refer to your particular pattern instructions before continuing too long, particularly if you need to secure the sewing to a mould.

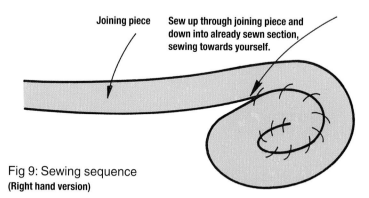

Joining piece

Sew up through joining piece and down into already sewn section, sewing towards yourself.

Fig 9: Sewing sequence
(Right hand version)

## INTRODUCING A NEW COLOUR

It is possible to introduce another colour into an item that is already under way, and there are two ways of doing this – the 'dead end' method, or the 'continuing' method. Both methods are suitable for all raffia projects, but you will need to take particular care if you are making a hat, for example, and want to use the dead end method. This method can create a slightly bulky feel, so you will have to incorporate the new colour carefully.

### Dead End Method

This method will completely finish one colour before you start using another, and is the trickier of the two methods to manoeuvre.

1. Plait and sew as normal with colour A. Continue sewing to the place where you would like to incorporate

colour B.

2. Approximately 6cm (2in) from this point, create a finishing bushy tail for colour A.

## Note:
Do not sew colour A right to the end of the plait.

3. Plait the necessary amount of colour B and create a starting bushy tail.

4. At colour B's joining place, secure B's starting bushy on the inside of the object, place B plait edge to edge with previous A row, and continue sewing.

## Note:
Make sure that you do not join B so close to its bushy that it can be seen from the outside of the object. In effect, you will be crossing A and B over on the inside of the object.

5. At the start of B, and for the final 6cm (2in) (to finish bushy of A), sew through both B and A to secure the tail end of the last colour.

Fig 10: Inside detail where dead-end method used to sew with two colour plaits

## Note:
It is your own choice as to whether you are now sewing in A or B.

6. When you have gone round the object once, you will be fully committed

with the new colour, so simply continue sewing the item as normal.

## Continuing Method

At the beginning of this method you will get the blend effect (see page 19).

1.    Plait with colour A following the normal four-knot instructions.

2.    At the place where you would like to start to introduce a different colour, gradually incorporate colour B knots where the previous strands weaken.

## Note:

You have the option here to carry on with both colours in either the blend or block options, or you can transfer completely to the new colour. If you intend to transfer completely to a new colour and you want this to happen at a particular place – for example, at the start of a hat brim – you will need to allow space to introduce the new colours as you can plait quite a distance before colour A has been completely taken over by colour B.

## SEWING CHECKLIST

1.    Always use good-quality, strong raffia – weak raffia will break too easily and this will mean more joining knots. As you sew with the raffia, it becomes weaker, so you need a strong piece to start with.

2.    Try to avoid forcing the plait to make sharp turns, especially at the beginning when the turns are particularly obtuse.

3.    Always pierce the pattern of the

plait; do not try to sew through a gap as, when you pull your stitch tighter, it will make this gap bigger.

4.    Use your sewing to close down any gaps you get.

5.    Do not worry unduly about doing particularly neat or small stitches – as you use raffia to sew the item together, your stitches will only be visible to you.

6.    Make sure you keep your plait edge to edge. Do not feel tempted to over- or under-lay the plait in the hope of closing down any gaps, as this will only make the item clumsy and bulky.

7.    To close down any gaps when you sew, simply pull your sewing a fraction tighter.

8.    Wherever possible (there are some exceptions), you should sew looking at the outside/top of the particular item.

9.    Always tie your new sewing thread on the inside/underneath, as you want the sewing knots to be out of sight.

10.    Do not trim the ends of the sewing knots closer than a minimum of 10mm (half an inch), as they may fray.

11.    When you have a new thread, make sure you follow the pattern of your previous stitching – up the joining plait and down through the already sewn section. If you sew the opposite way, this can buckle the item.

Above: Table mats showing (left to right) the dead end method and the continuing method of incorporating another colour. Note the distance that is covered on the continuing method before the second colour completely takes over.

# 6 Starting a Hat

This has proven to be the most popular part of any of the raffia craft work. The hats are not difficult to make, are extremely versatile, can be packed without fuss or bother (as roughly as you like), get wet, dry out and carry on as usual. They can be decorated with gay abandon or conservatively, and can also be remodelled if, for example, a matching outfit has had its day.

## ANATOMY OF A HAT

Throughout the instructions, I refer to different parts of the hats as shown in Fig 11.

## Top

This is the very top of the hat. It may be domed or flat, and in most cases is sewn flat before being stuck or pinned to the hat block.

## Sides

Once you have secured the hat to the block, you will start to sew down the sides of the block, creating the depth of the crown.

## Crown

The top and the sides together form the crown. This is the part of the hat that actually sits on the head.

## Crown Band

This is the last row of the crown and the part of the hat that may be lined if, for example, the feel of the raffia is uncomfortable. On the outside of the hat, this is the area which is most likely to be decorated, although there is no need to limit decoration to the band.

## Brim

This is the part of the hat that builds from the crown, the first row starting at 90 degrees from the crown. It may be large or small, depending on style, the size of the person and how much shade may be needed.

## HAT BLOCKS

One of the great advantages of raffia is that it is extremely pliable and this is particularly evident when working with a hat block to mould the crown of the hat. There

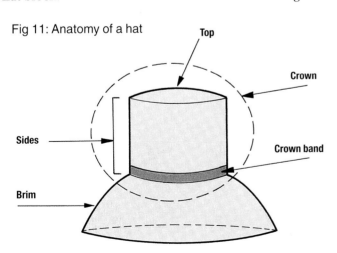

Fig 11: Anatomy of a hat

Top

Crown

Sides

Crown band

Brim

Opposite: The different stages of a hat.

Above: Various hat blocks – wooden, plaster and polystyrene.

are many materials, such as felt, which need to have a 'pure' mould (crown and brim), but with raffia this is not the case. Once a raffia hat is made and worn, the crown takes the shape of the head.

## Size and Fit

Although I know of milliners who do not always use blocks for their raffia hats, I do not recommend a free-style approach. For ease, and for a regular crown, the best option is to use a hat block. Before you can work with a block, however, it is essential to get the right size. If you do not have trouble getting a hat to fit in a high-street store, you are probably an industry standard 56cm (about 22in). However, if you are one of the many thousands of people who cannot get a hat to fit, you need to measure your head. Take a tape measure around your forehead (at the place where you would wear a sweatband) and check the size. The tape measure should stay above your ears and include the widest part of your crown at the back of your head.

Do not be tempted to use a block that is not going to produce a hat of the correct size. The blocks should be (but are not always) available to suit different sizes – I use 53cm (small, about 21in), 56cm (medium, about 22in), and 58.5cm (large, about 23in). If your required measurement is between sizes, with raffia you can still achieve the right fit, by bandaging the block to get the right size. If, for example, your head is 54.5cm (about 21in), buy a 53cm block and either use ordinary crepe bandage or an elastic thigh bandage to bring it up to the correct size. Raffia is such a flexible material that you do not need to worry that the block is not a perfect shape.

## Different Types of Block

Once you know the size you need, you will find out that there are many different types of hat blocks available (see photo, opposite). Wooden blocks are probably the best, but they can be difficult to source and are expensive. The beauty of working with wooden blocks is that they have a very nice feel, and they can be used to make hats using other materials if you do venture further into millinery. There are, however, cheaper options for making raffia hats that are just as efficient.

By far the most convenient and cheapest option is a polystyrene block. These are available in a small range of crown shapes; more importantly, check that the crown is sufficiently deep to allow for the correct hat depth.

## Making a Hat Block

You also have the option of making your own blocks; I have made blocks for myself and for use in my classes using casting plaster. Although the material is cheap to buy, it may be difficult to source – start with your local craft stores. The plaster can be messy, and it is also very fine and I would therefore

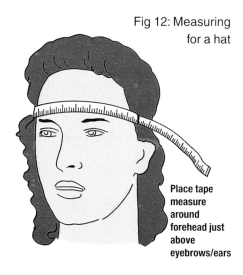

Fig 12: Measuring for a hat

**Place tape measure around forehead just above eyebrows/ears**

not recommend this method for asthmatics.

## EQUIPMENT

- about 2kg (4lb) of casting plaster
- crown of a hat in the correct size (do not use a good hat or one with a floppy crown; use either a raffia crown or an old hat)
- good amount of cling film
- four corks (these need not be new)
- four sharp tacks of medium length
- plastic mixing bowl
- approximately 1 litre (2 pints) of cold water
- pointed object, for example pencil or skewer
- hand-held whisk (not electric) (optional)
- tight-fitting gloves (for example, surgical)

## Note:

This method is not recommended for anyone who is at all asthmatic, as the dust produced is extremely fine and irritating. For this reason, it is also a good idea to work in a ventilated place. Additionally, make sure you will not be disturbed while you make the block, as

you need to work quickly before the plaster starts to set.

## INSTRUCTIONS

1.    Prepare the crown of your existing hat for the plaster by thoroughly lining the crown with cling film. Make sure that the cling film hangs over the edges of the crown, and use several layers so that you can be sure the plaster mix will not seep under and stick to the inside of the hat. If you do not put in enough cling film and this happens, the block and crown will be ruined.

2.    Place the four corks in the prepared hat in a square arrangement. Secure them in place by pinning from the outside of the crown, through the material of the hat and the cling film into the cork.

3.    Make sure that you keep this prepared crown close at hand ready to pour the plaster mixture into.

4.    With gloves on, place the plaster into the mixing bowl, with the water ready and the whisk (if using) near by.

5.    Add the water, slowly at first, and start stirring the mixture, either with your (gloved) hand or using the whisk. Add more water until all the mixture is stirred in and it resembles a thick yoghurt.

6.    Once the mixture is fully mixed, it will quite quickly start to set and get 'gloppier'. You need to pour it into the prepared hat crown at this stage. The ideal is for the mixture to fill the crown and not ooze

Opposite: The equipment needed for making a plaster hat block, with cling film already lining the crown to be filled.

**USEFUL TIP:**
Get into the habit of keeping new decisions in line with the bushy tail, for example, centring on the block, or creating the brim. This way, you make sure that all decisions are kept in one place – at the back of the hat.

**USEFUL TIP:**
If you use sellotape, as you sew around, simply go through the tape and remove any trace when you pull your crown off the block.

Opposite page: The first row of a hat brim. Note the 'X' on the block – the bushy tail mark. (This is the right-hand version.)

Right: With the hat fixed to a block, sewing through the joining piece towards myself on the top of the block (right-hand version).

between the layers of cling film. Leave the block to one side and let it set.

7.   Meanwhile, rinse the equipment you have used before it sets solid with plaster.

8.   Return to the drying block. You may decide to scratch a cross in the base of crown to show the bushy tail position before it sets too solidly. Ideally, the drying block is an oval, rather than a circular shape, either way you need to put a cross at one of the extreme ends of the oval to show the bushy tail mark (see photo, opposite).

9.   After about an hour you can remove the plaster from the crown. Take the tacks out and gently ease the plaster, with all cling film attached, from the hat crown. Over a rubbish bin, remove the cling film to leave only the plaster block.

10.   Leave the block in a cool place to dry through. As the plaster is so thick in the crown it will take quite a time (days) before it is completely dry, although it will actually be possible to use the block the day after you have made it.

## Note:

If you have not worked with casting plaster before, you might be surprised by the strange heat changes that occur when it starts to dry out. It is quite warm before it reaches a cool dry temperature. This is quite normal.

## CROWN AND START OF BRIM

As all the hat styles start in exactly the same way, the descriptions for the first stages are common to all styles. In most cases, only the final rows dictate a different style.

*EQUIPMENT*

- approximately 300–400g (10–14oz) raffia (use 400g for a dyed hat to allow for sewing and decorating)
- hat block
- sellotape or tacks
- needle

*INSTRUCTIONS*

1.   Plait approximately three-quarters of the raffia following the four-knot plait instructions. Secure the bushy tail.

2.   To start sewing you need to create the first turn; this will be an oval shape, to correspond to the shape of the head. This first turn needs to be approximately 5–6cm (2–2.25in) in length.

3.   Continue sewing around, following the sewing instructions on page 28, until the top of the crown is approximately the size of the top of the hat block you will be using, and your sewing is back level with the bushy tail.

4.   Before you secure your sewing to the block, you need to mark the base of the block to show the bushy tail

position. This cross needs to be at one or other end of the oval.

5.    Once you have marked the base of the block, fix the sewing to the top of the block (the top of the crown). This should be fixed bushy tail down, and bushy tail positioned directly over the mark on the base of the block. Depending on the block material, you can either fix with sellotape (on a polystyrene or wooden block), or secure with tacks if the block is wooden or plaster.

**USEFUL TIP:**
The crown is quite an easy part of the hat to sew. Before you were on the block you needed to sew from the top of the hat through to the inside (bushy tail side) and back through to the top again. Now you are on the block, you only need to pick up part of the joining and already sewn plaits, and secure the plait edge to edge (as before). It is not necessary to go completely through both pieces.

6.    Continue sewing around the crown, tight to the block. Your stitches should be from the joining plait (bottom part) through to the already sewn (top part), in other words, towards your body.

**USEFUL TIP:**
It is important to pull your stitches tighter on this part of the hat. If you pull too tightly when sewing off the block, the top of the crown buckles and does not stay flat. Now, as you want to maintain the correct size, you actually need to sew tight to the block. By pulling your stitches tighter, you can keep the correct size. Also, you cannot buckle the crown, as the plait can only become as tight as the block allows.

7.    Once you have sewn over the top of the block, and are on the sides of the crown, remember to move the hat block to a comfortable sewing position.

8.    Continue sewing around the block until you are approaching the bushy tail mark and the required depth of crown. If necessary, remove the hat from the block when you are level with the bushy tail and test it for size.

## Note:

Do not worry if your work does not seem to be of an even depth around the block. It is normal for it to be different depths, due either to the plait varying in width in different places; and/or to it not being attached to the top of the block in a completely central position. As long as it is not too shallow at the back or front of the hat, do not worry.

**USEFUL TIP:**
If you are uncertain about the correct depth of the crown, remove it from the block and try it on. The hat should rest just above the tops of your ears and not sit too high on the head. You do not want to feel that you have to hold it down to keep it on. If you are still uncertain, try sewing another row around and see if that is better. The rule is that you can always make it shallower, but it is much harder to make it deeper.

9.    Make sure your crown stays on the block (if you have taken it off to try on, make sure you secure it back in the correct position, with the bushy tail over the cross on the block), and sew to the bushy tail mark.

10.    To start sewing the brim, you will need to turn the block as if looking at the

**USEFUL TIP:**
Always keep your adjoining plait feeding in from the most obvious side – if you are right-handed, this will be on your left, and if left-handed it will be on the right. This helps prevent it getting twisted as you are sewing.

Opposite page: Bow decorations on a sun hat (left) and Breton (right).

Opposite: A selection of Breton hats, brim up and down.

inside of the hat, in other words, with the bottom of the block facing upwards (see photo page 37).

11. Using your left (right) hand to guide the plait around the block (do not pull the plait around), you will need to sew one row using an over stitch. Keeping the joining plait and the last row of the crown edge to edge, sew through both pieces. Your left (right) hand will be keeping the joining plait at a right-angle to the crown. Once again, because you are sewing tight to the block, you can keep these stitches tight.

12. Complete this right-angle row all the way around, and back to the bushy tail mark.

## Note:

As you get nearer to the bushy tail, you will notice that the previous row is 'pulling down' and is not flat to the block. Ignore this and continue the over stitch until you are back level with the bushy tail. You should end up ready to remove the complete crown from the

block and see that you have the first row of your brim already in place.

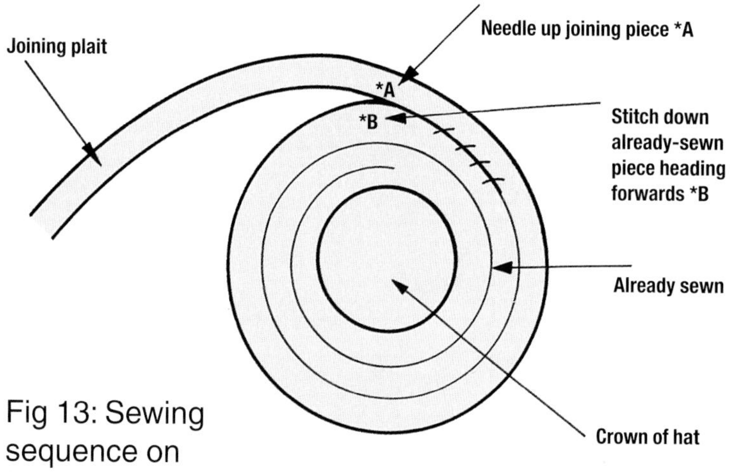

13. You can now continue with the brim. To do this, turn again to look at the outside of the hat and sew around, just as you sewed the top of the crown before you secured it to the block.

## Note:

The sequence of the sewing should be up through the joining piece and down through the already sewn part of the brim. Make sure you keep to this sequence (especially after knotting new threads), otherwise the brim of your hat may become buckled.

## Note:

Do not continue to pull the stitches as tight as you did on the block, as you will buckle the brim. You need to concentrate on bringing the plait edge to edge, and on pulling the stitches only tight enough to do this.

## Note:

The methods for adding new threads when sewing on the brim and crown are exactly the same. Pull your needle off on the inside of the hat, thread a new piece of raffia, and put your needle through the hat so that the old and new 'ends' are next to each other and can be tied. However, when you start sewing on the brim, make sure the remains of the knot are left neatly (either sewn down or threaded through the plait), so that they do not hang down in front of your face.

Remember always to get back into the correct sewing sequence when you thread a new piece of raffia – up the joining plait and down the already sewn plait. Before continuing too far on the size of your brim, refer to the different hat styles to decide how wide you would like your design.

**Joining plait**

**Needle up joining piece *A**

**Stitch down already-sewn piece heading forwards *B**

**Already sewn**

**Crown of hat**

Fig 13: Sewing sequence on brim

# 7 Hat Styles

## CHOOSING THE RIGHT STYLE

You may be one of those many people – and I am one of them – who do not consider themselves 'hat people', but would really like to wear them. Typically, this may be because your head is not an industry-standard size, and every style in the shops is too tight or too big; you may not be sure exactly how to wear a hat; or you may not know which style is better for you.

Making your own raffia hat solves the size dilemma – you can make your hat to the right size for you – see page 34, on making a hat block.

The solution to how to wear a hat is generally found through a simple manoeuvre – usually, the only mistake that people make is to wear it on the back of the head. Most hats, including the styles in this book, are designed to be worn more on the top of the head. Place the hat almost as if you want the crown band to touch your eyebrows at the front and the top of your ears around the sides. Finally, work the hat slightly back so that you do not have to crane your head to see anything.

Choosing the best style of hat for you is more personal. Whether you consider yourself a 'slave to fashion' or not, the right style will also be dictated by your face and body shape. A general rule is to choose a shape that does not exaggerate your 'worst' feature – avoid a wide hat for a wide face, or a tall hat for a long, narrow face, for example. Take a little time to experiment and find the hat style that works with your features. Wander through hat departments or shops, and try on as many different styles as possible to get an idea of the brim, size, scale and colour that might be best.

Creating your own hat gives you the opportunity to make it in a style, colour and finish that really flatter you.

## THREE BASIC HAT STYLES

There are three basic styles that I use most often – the sun hat, the Breton hat and the formal style. The most popular style among my students and my customers is probably the Breton, but each one of the styles makes an attractive and functional hat, with its own particular merits. The Breton is particularly versatile, as it can be worn with the brim either up or down for a different look.

Opposite: A selection of formal hats.

Below: A range of sun hats.

# The Sun Hat

The sun hat has a 'traditional' flat brim, and is probably the easiest style to make as, unlike the brim on the Breton and the formal styles, its brim requires no special turning to finish.

*INSTRUCTIONS*

1. Sew according to the basic hat start instructions. As you sew the brim, begin to assess the width you would like. This will vary from hat to hat, as the width of the plait and your personal choice vary. As a guide, the most popular adult width is 9–11cm (3–4in), or five to six brim rows.

## Note:
Remember this rule for getting the right brim width: you will always be able to make the hat smaller, but once you have cut the plait at the end it is extremely difficult to make the brim wider. Get used to trying the hat on while the brim is growing, in order to see the ideal width.

2. Stop level with the bushy tail at the beginning of the last row, as you need to consider the finishing of the hat.

3. Start the final row as normal and sew until you are approximately 20cm (8in) from being level with the bushy tail.

## Note:
You need to hide the plait gradually behind the previous row to stop the brim getting any bigger. You do not want to fade away too quickly, as this will make the edge of your hat uneven.

4. As you started the brim when you were level with the bushy tail, you need to finish the brim level with the bushy tail. Leaving the plait slack enough to complete the final section of the row, use a peg to hide the plait completely behind the previous row just past the bushy tail mark.

5. You should find that the remaining part of the plait falls into an even curve up to the bushy tail mark. You need to ensure that this final section keeps the brim even while still gradually hiding behind the previous row. Use pegs to help get a regular brim finish.

6. Sew this section to approximately 4cm (1in) past the bushy tail mark, keeping the joining plait completely

> **USEFUL TIP:**
> You might find it helps to place a peg on the brim of the hat 20cm (8in) from the bushy tail, so that you do not sew too far.

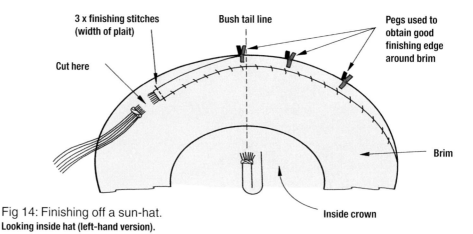

Fig 14: Finishing off a sun-hat.
**Looking inside hat (left-hand version).**

hidden behind the previous row. Where the previous row overlaps the joining section, simply sew through both pieces.

## Note:

As you sew near the extreme edge of the brim, avoid the temptation to sew over the edge, but continue to stitch the width of the joining plait.

7.    The next stage is to secure the width of the plait to the brim. Sew three small stitches the width of the final piece of plait, so that not the whole plait is held to the brim. Remove your needle, leave the remaining sewing thread hanging.

## Note:

Although this is the final part of the hat, you should ideally have at least 6cm (2in) of thread remaining.

8.    Take a healthy new raffia thread. Manoeuvre it underneath the section of plait you have just secured, as far as the small stitches you have just sewn.

9.    With the new thread and the remains of your old sewing thread, tie a secure double knot, pulling the plait tight together, creating a bushy tail. Cut the old and new threads from the plait. (See photo page 47, as a guide.)

10.   Cut the plait (being very careful not to cut the brim of the hat) about 1.5cm (0.5in) from the knot at the attached

### USEFUL TIP:

If you still have a considerable amount of plait attached, take the new thread and place it approximately 3cm (just over 1in) further along the plait. Secure a further double knot and leave the thread hanging.

piece of plait (between the two knots, if you have extra plait). You should leave a finishing bushy tail attached to the hat, and possibly a new starting bushy tail for another project.

## The Breton Hat

1.    Sew according to the basic hat start instructions. As you sew the brim, begin to assess the width you would like. This will vary from hat to hat, with the width of a plait and personal choice. As a guide, the most popular total brim width (adult size) is 8–9cm (3–3in), or five to six brim rows in total.

## Note:

Remember, you will always be able to make the hat smaller, but once you have cut the plait at the end it is extremely difficult to make the brim wider. Try the hat on while the brim is growing to see the ideal width.

Left: Selection of Breton hats, with brims both up and down.

Right: Finishing the Breton hat, with the brim in the up position. Use pegs evenly to fade away the plait inside the brim (pointing towards the outside of the crown).

## Note:

For the Breton style, you need to decide if you intend to wear the hat with the brim up. For a five-row brim this means there will be three rows flat on the brim, while the fourth and fifth rows create the turn-up.

2.    Once you have decided the width of brim you would like, stop level with the bushy tail at the beginning of the last row.

3.    The final row of the Breton hat is sewn with the last row completely underneath (the previous row of the brim pointing towards the inside of the hat).

## Note:

Do not worry that this may look a strange way to finish the Breton, this method provides a sort of 'hinged' effect to the final style.

4.    Using your left (right) hand to hold the joining plait in place, start sewing an over-stitch all the way along the outside edge of the brim.

**USEFUL TIP:**

Place a peg on the brim of the hat 10cm (4in) from the bushy tail, so that you do not sew too far.

5.    Continue like this until you are approximately 10cm (4in) from being level with the bushy tail.

6.    At this point, turn the brim of the hat up into the Breton shape. Finish the last part of this style with the brim in this position.

7.    As you started the brim when you were level with the bushy tail, you need to finish the brim level with the bushy tail. Leaving the plait slack enough to complete the final section of the row, use a peg to completely hide the plait behind the previous row just past the bushy tail mark. On the Breton style, this means you finish the plait on the inside part of the upturned brim, with the bushy tail facing the outside back of the crown (see photo opposite).

8.    You should find that the remaining part of the plait will fall into a straightish edge along the top of the upturned brim, to the bushy tail mark. You need to ensure that this final section keeps a smooth, straight edge to the brim, while gradually hiding the joining plait behind the previous row. Use pegs to achieve a regular finish.

9.    Sew this section to approximately 4cm (1in) past the bushy tail mark, keeping the joining plait completely hidden behind the previous row. Where the previous row overlaps the joining section, simply sew through both pieces.

## Note:

As you sew near the extreme edge of the brim, avoid the temptation to sew over the edge, but continue to stitch across the width of the joining plait.

10.    The next stage is to secure the width of the plait to the brim. Sew three small stitches the width of the final

piece of plait, so that more than one section of the plait is held to the brim, showing a similar idea for finishing the sun hat). Remove your needle, leave the remaining sewing thread hanging.

## Note:

Although this is the final part of the hat, you should ideally have at least 6cm (2in) of thread remaining.

11.   Take a healthy new raffia thread. Manoeuvre it underneath the section of plait you have just secured, as far as the small stitches you have just sewn.

12.   With the new thread and the remains of your old sewing thread, tie a secure double knot, pulling the plait tight together, creating a bushy tail. Cut the old and new threads from the plait.

13.   Cut the plait (being very careful not to cut the brim of the hat) about 1.5cm (0.5in) from the knot at the attached piece of plait (between the two knots if you have extra plait). You should leave a finishing bushy tail attached to the hat, and possibly a new starting bushy tail for another project.

## The Formal Hat

This style is a variation on the sun hat, providing a smarter edge to the brim, and, as its name suggests, a more formal look for a wedding, for example.

1.   Sew according to the basic hat start instructions. As you sew the brim, begin to assess the width you would like. This will vary from hat to hat, with the width of a plait and personal choice. As a guide, the most popular total brim width (adult size) is 8–9cm (3–3.25in), or five to six brim rows in total.

## Note:

Remember, you will always be able to make the hat smaller, but once you have cut the plait at the end it is extremely difficult to make the brim wider. Try the hat on while the brim is growing to see the ideal width.

2.   Sew the brim of this style to the required width and stop level with the bushy tail.

3.   The final row of the formal hat is sewn with the last row completely on top of the previous row of the brim (pointing towards the outside of the crown).

4.   Using your left (right) hand to hold the joining plait in place, start sewing an over-stitch along the outside edge of the brim.

Left: With a new thread and the finish of the old sewing thread, getting ready to tie the final bushy tail. The remaining plait is then cut from the Breton style.

Right: The final row of the formal hat, with the row on the top of hat pointing towards the outside of the crown.

5. Continue like this until you are back level with the bushy tail, at the place where you started the final row.

6. Now you need to finish off this last row. To do this, sandwich the joining plait between the gap created by the upturned last row and the last flat row of the brim. Sew only through the joining plait and the upturned last row – do not sew to the last flat row of the brim.

**Note:**
If you sew through all parts of the 'sandwich', this will prevent the upturned row standing up after you have pressed the brim.

7. Continue sewing for approximately 5cm (2in), forcing the joining plait to disappear between the 'row sandwich'.

**Note:**
This is to avoid abruptly stopping your sewing, although you are not so concerned with 'gently' finishing the row as you would be for the sun hat or the Breton hat.

8. Once the joining plait is completely hidden, you need to secure the width of the plait to the top row of the brim. Sew three small stitches the width of the final piece of plait, so that more than one section of the plait is held to the row, showing a similar idea for finishing the sun hat). Remove your needle, leave the remaining sewing thread hanging.

**Note:**
Although this is the final part of the hat, you should ideally have at least 6cm (2in) of thread remaining.

9. Take a new healthy raffia thread. Manoeuvre it underneath the section of plait you have just secured, as far as the small stitches you have just sewn.

10. With the new thread and the remains of your old sewing thread, tie a secure double knot, pulling the plait tight together, creating a bushy tail. Cut the old and new threads from the plait.

11. Cut the plait (being very careful not to cut the brim of the hat) approximately 1.5cm (0.5in) from the knot at the attached piece of plait (between the two knots if you have extra plait). You should leave a finishing bushy tail attached to the hat, and possibly a new starting bushy tail for another project.

## OTHER STYLES

There are many different hat styles that could be produced using raffia; you need to experiment to see how a style works with the material. Following are two more suggestions.

## Sewn-Back Sun Hat

This style is ideal for a small child, as it gives the option of making a pretty hat that will also provide the shade that is so important.

## Note:

Iron this hat before you finalize the brim style, as it will not be so easy to do once the brim is sewn in place.

This is an adaptation of the basic sun hat style. Make a sun hat to the required size, but keep in mind that you will be securing back one side of the brim, so you will not want to make it too narrow. Once the hat is complete, you sew back either the front or the back of the brim.

I recommend you sew back the back of the hat – the part where the bushy tail is finished. This way, the wearer can choose to have the brim at the front (without having the bushy tail in their line of vision), or at the back. Before sewing back the bushy tail part of the brim, you will need to make sure that you will be able to disguise the tail when you are decorating the hat.

## Cloche Hat

This very stylish hat gets its name from the French word for 'bell'. It is similar in shape to the Breton, but with the brim sewn permanently down, giving it a bell-like shape.

A word of warning – it is quite difficult to sew a regular bell shape around the brim and, once the hat is complete, it can also be difficult to keep it looking smart. This style does not survive being rolled up in a suitcase quite as well as the other styles. Try making some other styles before attempting to make the cloche, as you really need to have mastered the basics.

To complete a cloche, you need to sew the basic crown shape as for all the other hat styles. For the brim, sew the first row as for all others – at right-angles to the block and the crown of the hat.

For the rest of the brim, carefully and gradually sew at an angle to create the bell shape. The basic principle of sewing around the hat until you have achieved the required width of brim is exactly the same, only the shape differs. If your heart is set on this style, take care and be patient, and be prepared to unpick a row if necessary and try again.

## Note:

As with the sewn-back sun hat, I recommend you iron a cloche hat before you decorate it, particularly if you like the idea of sewing ribbon completely around the brim.

Far left: Creating the sewn-back sun hat. Note that the bushy tail is evident (just below my right thumb), which shows this is the back of the brim.

Left: Decorating the sewn-back sun hat, and disguising the bushy tail at the same time.

## FANCY A CHANGE?

I have frequently mentioned the versatility of raffia. This adaptability gives you almost limitless options for changing and updating hats, something that I did many times in my early hat-making days!

You may have made a formal hat to wear at a wedding. Now that the occasion has passed, or perhaps the outfit has long been discarded, you have the opportunity to remove the ribbon or decorations (which should only be lightly sewn in place), unpick the last row of the hat, re-sew it as a Breton or sun hat, fix new trimming, re-press the brim of the hat to secure the new style and – hey presto – you have a new garden hat, beach hat or casual hat. You will be amazed at how easily this is done.

This option is also ideal for the sewn-back sun hat. If a little girl has grown out of the style, you can simply unpick the secured brim, and re-press the hat flat to give a sun hat. Alternatively, extend the hat with another colour plait (see page 30), for the 'dead end' method of adding a new colour) to make a Breton hat, re-press it and put it into shape.

This remodelling option applies to all hat styles. Simply take care in unpicking your plait – only cut your stitches – and make sure you re-press the hat once you have re-sewn it. You need to make sure also that you use fresh raffia to sew the new style, as the sewing thread you unpick will be frayed and unsuitable for re-use.

## IRONING YOUR HAT

Although it is not essential to iron your hats, it gives them a more professional finish and helps them to hold their shape longer. If you decide to iron your hat, do this before you finalize or attach any decorative trims. If you need to re-iron a hat, remove any detachable trims, and work very carefully around any that are permanent.

The basic ironing technique is similar for every style, and for each hat the crown is always done exactly the same. The brim, however, is ironed differently depending on the style – the golden rule is to 'iron as you have sewn'. Follow the basic instructions below for the crown, and then choose the option according to the style you have made.

A raffia hat is very durable, and you will find that if you go swimming in yours, or pack it tightly in a suitcase, or get caught in the rain, it will not suffer. All you will need to do is make sure it dries

Below: Left to right: a cloche hat and a sewn-back sun hat.

naturally and thoroughly, then simply re-iron the whole hat (although it is likely that only the brim will need re-shaping). Your hat will soon be as good as new.

## Ironing the Crown

*EQUIPMENT*

(The equipment is the same for all hat styles.)

- ordinary household steam iron
- ironing board or other flat surface
- bowl of warm water
- old tea cloth or similar (a slightly thinner, older cloth is better than a new one)
- hat block

*INSTRUCTIONS*

1.    Half-fill the steam chamber of the iron and put the dial on the full heat and steam setting.

2.    Place the hat block inside the crown of the hat.

3.    Completely wet the tea cloth and wring out excess water – do not wring the tea cloth entirely dry – you will need some moisture in it.

4.    Place the hat on the ironing board or flat surface.

5.    Cover the crown of the hat with the damp cloth, making sure the entire surface is covered.

6.    Press the hot steam iron on top of the cloth, making sure that the top and sides of the (covered) crown make contact with the hot iron. If necessary, re-moisten the cloth so that a fresh wet

Left: Place the hat on the block before you press the crown.

piece is pressed each time.

7.    Replace the cloth in the water to re-moisten it, and remove the hat block from the crown of the hat.

## Note:

If you have used a particularly flat-domed block and you would like a more 'rounded' crown, it is a good idea to place the hat on your head while it is still slightly damp and warm from the ironing. This will not damage the hat in any way and you will immediately see the crown take a rounder look.

## Ironing the Brim

After you have ironed the crown you will need to press the brim, following the instructions for the style of hat you have chosen.

## Sun Hat (and Sewn-Back Sun Hat)

This is the easiest style to press, since the brim has been sewn without any overlapping or under-lapping of the plait.

Right: Steam iron a fresh damp piece of cloth on each part of the crown.

1.    With your (newly) wet cloth, place a fresh wet piece on each section of the brim and press firmly. If your cloth starts to dry out, wet it again, otherwise the results will not be even.

2.    As you turn the brim to each new section, make sure that you are not buckling or bending the section you have just pressed as you progress, especially if you have a particularly wide brim that may be overlapping the edges of your ironing board.

3.    Once you have worked completely around the brim, it is best to leave the hat to 'rest' on a dry, flat surface.

Right: Pressing the brim of a hat (here, a formal style).

As there is no additional embellishment to this brim, it is likely that it will become more easily buckled and damaged with hard wear. Simply repeat the brim pressing whenever you feel like giving the hat a fresher look.

## Breton Hat

The technique for ironing this style of hat starts to illustrate the 'iron as sewn' principle.

1.    In making this brim, you have sewn the last row under the previous row – in other words, you have turned it towards the inside of the crown. Before you can iron the brim you need to turn the last row under, back into the original sewing position. You will note that the weight of the bushy tail may try to push the final few centimetres of the plait upwards, so make sure that it remains in the 'under' position.

2.    With your (newly) wet cloth, and making sure that the last row of the plait remains under, place a fresh wet piece on each section of the brim and press firmly.

3.    If your cloth starts to dry out, take time to wet it again, otherwise the results will not be even.

### Note:

If you iron a section wrongly, with the last row curled on the outside, simply re-wet the cloth and re-iron the section.

4.    Once you have worked completely around the brim, and ideally while the brim is still slightly damp or warm, you need to shape it into its

intended Breton style by uncurling the folded row and moulding it upwards.

5.   While the brim starts to dry and cool, continue turning the brim into the required shape.

6.   Leave the hat to cool and dry thoroughly for a few minutes on a flat surface.

## Note:

Even if you do not intend always to wear the hat with the brim upwards, which is one of the appealing options of the Breton, it is still best to store it in this position.

## Formal Hat

1.   When ironing this hat, you should keep the last row of plaiting on top of the brim and pointing towards the outside of the crown – as it was sewn.

2.   With your (newly) wet cloth, place a fresh wet piece on each section of the brim and press firmly. If your cloth starts to dry out, take time to wet it again, otherwise the results will not be even.

3.   Once you have ironed every part, and ideally while the brim is still slightly damp or warm, run your fingers around the brim, gently lifting the last row into a more upright position, so that it is standing proud. This gives the final row a more pronounced appearance, if preferred.

4.   Leave the hat to cool for a few minutes on a flat, dry surface.

## Cloche Hat

Ironing this type of hat is not very different from ironing the sun hat, except that you must not place the brim of the cloche flat on the ironing board, as this defies its design. Instead, to press the brim, you have to do it gently, piece by piece, hanging it off the end of the ironing board.

1.   Position the hat so that the end of your board is just touching the start of the brim, pointing towards the inside of the crown and about one-sixth of the brim is actually on the board.

2.   With your (newly) wet cloth, place a fresh wet piece on this section of the brim and press firmly. Remove the cloth and turn the brim so that the next sixth of the brim is on the board.

3.   Repeat step 2, until all sections of the brim have been pressed. If your cloth starts to dry out, take time to wet it again, otherwise the results will not be even.

4.   Once you have ironed every part, find a position to let the hat cool. This style needs to be left 'hung', so that the brim does not become flattened.

# 8 Bags

Once you have mastered the basic plaiting technique, and have realized how pliable raffia is, you will quickly see how wide is the range of goods you can create with raffia work – each individually made to your own colour, shape and style requirements. Among the most useful of these items are a multitude of bags, suitable for many different occasions.

The size of the bags you can make with raffia is only limited by the items you might want to carry in them. Raffia has little intrinsic strength, so that a bigger bag made of raffia does not necessarily have a greater carrying power than a smaller one. I have, therefore, made suggestions here for ways in which larger items may be reinforced, so that you can carry heavier goods. Without reinforcement to the bag, several kilos of groceries or books will force the bottom of a large raffia bag to sag and, not only will it feel and look ungainly, it will also be insecure. I have suggested strengthening that is in keeping with the appearance of each item, and yet provides ample reinforcement.

Opposite: Colourful practicality: a beach bag (left), and bucket bag.

Right: a circular handbag (left) and a beach bag (showing a reinforced 'skirt' on the outside).

## BEACH BAG

Although the name suggests towels, costumes, insect repellent and sandy sandwiches, this is an extremely versatile bag and, depending upon the level of strengthening, can be used for much more.

## The Bag

*EQUIPMENT*

(For a bag 124cm (49in) in circumference, and 36cm (14in) deep.)

- approximately 600g (21oz) of raffia (you can use up the different pieces of colour left over from other items)
- mould (for example, a plastic laundry basket)
- needle
- sellotape or parcel tape
- pegs to secure handles in place for sewing

*INSTRUCTIONS*

1. Knot, plait and trim approximately three-quarters of the raffia following the instructions for the five-thread, four-knot plait.

2. Start sewing your plait, ensuring that the first turn that you make with your bushy tail corresponds with the shape of the base of your mould. For example, if your base is circular, you will need to create a very sharp (circular) turn with your bushy tail.

3. Continue sewing to the shape of your base until you are level with your bushy tail and you have a shape approximately the same size as the base of your mould.

4. Fix the sewn raffia to the base of the mould, ensuring that you have a mark somewhere on the mould which signifies the place for the bushy tail. (For example, you could stick a piece of raffia on to one of the handles of the laundry basket.) Make sure that you will not be covering this mark while you continue to sew, as it is always important to be able to quickly identify where your bushy tail is.

5. Continue sewing the plait until you have covered your mould, plaiting more knots as you need to.

6. On your last row, and approximately 10cm (4in) from your bushy tail mark, remove the bag from the mould.

7. To finish the bag you need to 'hide' the plait behind the previous row. Gradually taper the plait away, inside the bag, so that the top edge is as straight as possible. Note that you should have completely finished placing the plait behind by the time you are just past the bushy tail, otherwise you have, in effect, started the next row.

8. Secure the final section by sewing three small stitches the width of the plait – this stops the plait being secured in only one part of the plait (see Fig 14, page 44, for the same principle used when finishing sun hat). Remove your needle, but leave the end of your sewing thread untrimmed.

9. Place a new strand of raffia underneath your plait and pull it close to the last piece you have sewn.

10. Using the sewing thread left in place, and the new strand of raffia, tie a tight double knot, and cut the old and new strands close to these knots.

12. Approximately 2cm (just under an inch) from the trimmed knots, cut the remainder of your plait, being careful not to cut through the final row of the bag. This should leave a secure bushy tail attached to the bag, plus a bushy tail ready to begin making the

handles or for another project if you wish.

## The Handles

There are a number of different options for the handles for this bag, some of which may provide additional strength. The basic length of the handles should be 100cm (40in), with over 50cm (20in) attached inside the bag. To add the very minimum of strengthening for this bag, attach reinforcements to the handles. One of the nice features of these bags is that, if the handles get worn, or if you feel like a change of colour, you can easily insert new handles without having to unpick the whole bag.

1.  Plait a minimum of 200cm (80in) to allow for two handles.

2.  Secure the ends, as if creating bushy tails ready to sew. Take two good pieces of raffia and tie them approximately 5cm (2in) apart in the middle of the plait, then cut the length of plait evenly into two. You should be left with two pieces of even length that have neat bushy tails at both ends.

3.  Plait approximately 80cm (32in) to allow for two small handles (for reinforcement), and secure and cut according to the instructions for long handles.

4.  Find the middle point of one of the long handles, and of one of the small handles. Match these middle points, putting the trimmed side of the two handles together. Sew the smaller handle to the larger before you fix them to the bag, as this makes a much neater job.

5.  Repeat step 4 for the other handle.

6.  Using the pegs, position the handles (with the reinforced parts already attached) inside or outside the bag, whichever you prefer. Take time to place the handles an even distance apart and within the circumference of the bag, to avoid a lop-sided bag. If you have used a circular mould, you can also position the handles so that they

disguise the finishing bushy tail of your plait on the top row of the bag.

7. Start to sew the handles firmly in place. Take time to sew them securely, particularly at their base and at the top of the bag.

## REINFORCEMENTS

The beach bag is a very popular style of bag, so I have included more than one idea for reinforcing it, some of which could be combined to come up with a really tough finished item.

## Bag 'Skirt'

*EQUIPMENT*

- approximately 200g (7oz) raffia for a 'skirt' approximately 7cm (about 3in) deep
- completed bag (ideally still in place on the mould)
- sellotape, parcel tape or tacks

*INSTRUCTIONS*

1. Plait the raffia, keeping enough available for sewing the skirt.

2. Start to sew the 'skirt', following the instructions for the beginning of the base of the bag. Continue sewing until you have a shape large enough to cover the base of the bag.

3. Attach the skirt to the bag, which is on the mould, positioning the bushy tail in line with the mark on your mould. It is important to sew the skirt over the bag while it is on the mould to get the correct size, as the skirt needs to be slightly bigger than the bag.

4. Continue sewing, as if creating a new bag over the existing one. You have the option of either sewing through both the skirt and the bag (use a curved needle for this), or sewing only the skirt. If you sew only the skirt, you can easily remove and replace it with a new one if it becomes worn on the base.

5. Sew the skirt as deep as you require.

6. To finish the skirt, follow the beach bag instructions, steps 7-11.

7. Remove the bag and the skirt from the mould and sew around the edge of the skirt, securing it to the bag.

## Variations on the 'Skirt'

Repeat the beginning stages of the beach bag to make the 'skirt', and secure it direct to the mould (rather than to the bag, as above). With this method you start to make another bag, partially as deep as the original, which you can sew or place inside the bag, for a 'petticoat' reinforcement.

Alternatively, you can create a 'skirt' first – there is no need to finish the edge of the plait tidily for this method – keep it on the mould, and then start to create the bag. Attach the bag to the mould, on top of the skirt, and sew through both the skirt and the bag as normal. This way, you do not have to go back and secure the skirt in place.

## Reinforced Base

This method provides an extra layer inside the base of the bag, and is extremely simple to make. You can use natural raffia when you make a

Opposite: Use pegs to hold the handles in place while they are sewn into the beach bag. Note the natural-coloured base – this is a reinforced base, and not the real bottom of the bag.

reinforced base, as it seems wasteful to use dyed raffia when it is not going to be seen.

*EQUIPMENT*

- approximately 100g (3oz) raffia for a base about 31cm (12in) in diameter (to fit the beach bag described earlier)
- mould, or the finished bag you want to reinforce

*INSTRUCTIONS*

1. Repeat steps 1 and 2 of the instructions for the base of the beach bag.

2. Continue sewing to the shape of your base until you have achieved nearly the same size as the base of the finished bag.

3. Finish the sewing according to steps 7–11 in the instructions for the beach bag.

4. You should be left with a flat base, like a table mat, which you can place inside the bag to reinforce the bottom.

## BUCKET BAG

This bucket-shaped bag can be made either as a shoulder bag or in a hand-held version.

*EQUIPMENT*

(For a bag 78cm (31in) in circumference, and 23cm (9in) deep.)

- approximately 250g (8oz) of raffia
- mould (a bucket is good!)

- needle
- sellotape or parcel tape
- pegs to secure handles in place for sewing

This is a smaller version of the beach bag, and the instructions for making it are exactly the same, although the mould gives a different shape. Follow steps 1–11 given in the instructions for the beach bag. As the bucket bag is smaller, any reinforcements will probably not need to be as sturdy as for the beach bag, but it is a good idea to secure a reinforced base to all your bags.

## ATTACHÉ BAG

*EQUIPMENT*

(For a bag 28cm (11in) high, 41cm (16in) wide, and 16cm (6in) deep.)

- approximately 450g (15oz) of raffia
- rectangular mould (I used two tomato boxes taped together and used sideways)
- needle
- sellotape and parcel tape
- pegs to secure handles in place for sewing

## Note:

As with all bags, the handles need to be long enough to cope with the contents. The handles for this bag should be approximately 50cm (20in) each, and can be attached on the inside or the outside of the bag.

The principles involved in making this bag are exactly the same as for the beach bag, with the exception of the first turn that is needed to fix on the mould. Working to a rectangular shape needs particular care, and you should be

Opposite: Small attaché bag (plaited with raffia and seagrass), plus other projects.

Above: attaché bag (left), and small attaché bag plaited with seagrass and raffia (right).

prepared not to get it right first time.

You need to create a first turn that causes the width of your base to grow at a corresponding rate to the length. This is not a problem for a circular pattern. However, if you do not take care on a rectangular mould, and make the first turn too long (or too short), you will quickly exceed the length of the base without having sewn to the width of the base, and vice versa. Unfortunately, there is no 'magic formula', and you will need to learn through trial and error.

Once you get past the first stage, continue sewing the bag on the mould and follow the instructions for the beach bag (from step 3) for finishing and securing your joining plait. Complete the handles either on the outside or inside of the bag as with the beach bag handles.

## SMALL ATTACHÉ BAG

*EQUIPMENT*

(For a bag 22cm (9in) high, 27cm (11in) wide, 15cm (6in) deep.)

◆ approximately 300g (10oz) of raffia

Opposite: Circular handbag.

◆ rectangular mould (I used a small 6-bottle wine box)
◆ needle
◆ sellotape or parcel tape
◆ pegs to secure handles in place for sewing

Again, the handles need to be long enough to cope with the weight of the contents, and these should be approximately 50cm (20in) each. For the small version of the attaché bag, follow the same instructions, but using a different mould. Remember to take care over the first turn needed to secure to the mould.

## CIRCULAR HANDBAG

This is more of a 'lipstick and credit card' style than a basket like the others. It can be a casual item to match a hat, or is perfect for a young girl. This version has a small handle, but the style would work equally well with a larger handle.

*EQUIPMENT*

(For a bag measuring 23cm (9in) in diameter.)

- approximately 200g (7oz) raffia
- needle
- material for lining (optional)
- fastener (optional)

*INSTRUCTIONS*

1.    Plait the raffia, leaving an amount spare for sewing, and to create a fastener if required.

2.    Create two circular table-mat shapes approximately 23cm (9in) in diameter. You may need to do some clever manoeuvring to make these exactly the same size.

3.    You should be left with a plait that measures no less than about 170cm (68in). This one piece will form your handle. Create a bushy tail at either end of the plait.

4.    Curl the length of plait into a circle, so that the bushy tails are 'nose-to-nose', and inside the circle.

5.    Keeping the circle shape, sew the plait edge to edge, making sure the width of this circle is even – double plait width – all the way around. To do this, you will need to overlap the bushy tails to the inside of the circle. Once sewn, this circle will form the base of the bag, as well as the sides and the handle.

6.    Keeping the bushy tails (of the handle) at the bottom of the bag, rest one of the 'table mats' in the curve of the handle, and sew the handle and 'mat' edge to edge for about two-thirds of the

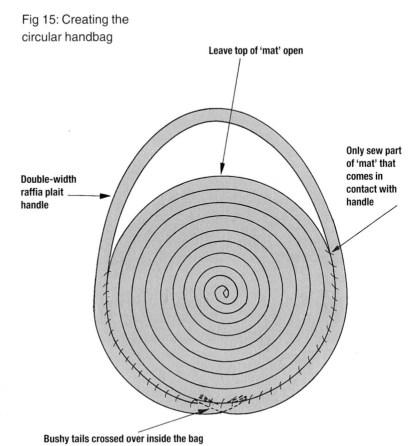

Fig 15: Creating the circular handbag

Leave top of 'mat' open

Double-width raffia plait handle

Only sew part of 'mat' that comes in contact with handle

Bushy tails crossed over inside the bag

circle, leaving the top section open.

7.    Repeat this for the second 'mat', sewing the same area as before.

8.    At the height of the handle grip, sew the two edges of the (double) plait together – this makes it more tubular and more comfortable to carry.

9.    Material for lining the bag is optional, but, if you intend to carry small items, lining is essential to avoid losing anything out of any gaps. A fastener is also a good idea; you could use a favourite button, a twist of raffia, or an attractive tassel.

# 9 Home Accessories

With the increasing interest in such disciplines as Feng Shui, and in generally streamlining and downsizing our lifestyle, it has become key to throw out excess belongings, and to keep the house in order. Storage is a problem for many people, and here raffia can come to the rescue.

Using everyday items as a basis, with raffia you can make many attractive and practical items, large or small, for your home. The more I work with raffia and create new ideas, the more I think that the options are limitless.

The basic technique is very similar for many of the items. The difficult part can be sourcing a good mould on which to build the items – I scour the charity shops and do not throw out any old jars or containers.

For those items that only show a materials list and mould ideas, follow the basic instructions below. Specific instructions are included where they are needed.

## BASIC INSTRUCTIONS

1. Knot, plait and trim approximately three-quarters of your raffia as for the five-thread, four-knot plait. Create a bushy tail at the start of your plait.

2. Make sure there is a mark or position on your mould that you can use as a bushy tail 'position'.

3. Depending on the shape of your mould, create your first turn. Continue sewing until you are level with your bushy tail and you have a shape approximately the same size as the base of your mould.

4. Fix your sewing to the base of the mould, keeping your bushy tail in line with the mark on your mould. Avoid covering this mark as you continue to sew around.

5. Continue sewing the plait until you have covered your mould, plaiting more knots as you need to.

6. When you reach your last row, and are approximately 10cm (4in) from your bushy tail mark, remove the object from the mould.

7. To finish the item you need to 'hide' the plait behind the previous row. Gradually taper the plait away, inside the shape, so that the top edge is as straight a line as possible. Note that you should have completely finished placing the plait behind by the time you are just past the bushy tail, otherwise you will, in effect, have started the next row.

8. Secure the final section by sewing three small stitches the width of the plait, so that the plait is not secured only in one part. Remove your needle, but leave the end of your sewing thread untrimmed.

9. Place a new strand of raffia underneath your plait and pull it close to the last piece you have sewn.

Opposite top: Stylish vase (left) – note how it is a 'sleeve' on the container); other containers showing base options.

Opposite far left: Twist and tie lampshade (left), and vertical lampshade (right).

Opposite right: Photo frame options.

10. Using the sewing thread left in place, and the new strand of raffia, tie a tight double knot and cut the old and new strands close to these knots.

11. Approximately 2cm (just under an inch) from the trimmed knots, cut the remainder of your plait, being careful not to cut through the final row of the object. This should leave a secure bushy tail attached to the object, plus a bushy tail ready to begin making another project if you wish.

## LOG BASKET

This is the largest raffia item I have ever made; it definitely needs adequate support if you plan to move it around or carry the logs in it.

*EQUIPMENT*

(For a basket 131cm (52in) in circumference, 31cm (12in) deep.)

- approximately 600g (21oz) raffia
- needle and tape
- mould (I used the 'muck' bucket that I use for dyeing)
- lightweight board or wood
- about 15 supports, for example, flower sticks
- glue gun

*INSTRUCTIONS*

Follow steps 1 to 11 of the basic instructions. The handles on the log basket need to be approximately 75cm (30in) each, fixed to the outside of the basket. The basket can be strengthened by using a piece of lightweight board or wood cut to size and put in the basket, and flower sticks stuck to the inside.

## WASTE-PAPER BASKET OR DRIED-FLOWER BASKET

*EQUIPMENT*

(For a basket 85cm (34in) in circumference, 23cm (9in) deep.)

- approximately 200g (7oz) raffia
- needle and tape
- mould (either a bucket or an old waste-paper basket)
- material for lining the inside of the basket (optional)
- supports, for example, flower sticks (optional)
- glue gun

*INSTRUCTIONS*

Follow the basic instructions. Although this item is smaller than the log basket, and will probably not carry the same amount of weight, you might still choose to strengthen the sides. For this, use smaller green garden sticks, stuck

Below: log basket (right, showing the supports attached inside) and the 'muck' bucket mould used for making it (left). Note the floor mat under the log basket.

Far left: Waste-paper or dried-flower basket.

Left: A selection of pots and containers.

Below: A selection of pots and containers, all using the five-thread knot method, with the exception of the small pink pencil pot.

together in pairs, and fixed occasionally around the basket.

## POTS AND CONTAINERS

Depending on the final purpose of the pot, there are two methods – the usual five-thread knots, or, for a less rigid pot with a different finish, the lighter method. The lighter method uses only two raffia threads per knot, instead of making the knots with five threads. This makes a much thinner plait (there are only eight threads across the whole plait, instead of twenty), and it also means that it takes longer to make an item of similar size than it does with a five-thread plait. The resultant pots and containers, although lightweight, are functional, and can be made quite large and still be practical.

You also have the option of keeping a 'lining' in the pot or container. This makes the pot particularly rigid, and can also make it waterproof, which may be very useful. Generally, you are only limited in the size you can create by how much you want the item to stand upright, or to hold.

## Shaker-Style Candle Holder

Hung on a hook, this is not only a useful way to keep candles at hand, but perfect for using up oddments, as it takes only a very small amount of raffia.

*EQUIPMENT*

(For a holder 15cm (6in) deep, 30cm (12in) in circumference.)

◆ approximately 100g (3oz) raffia
◆ mould (for example, a small lemonade bottle)
◆ needle and sellotape

*INSTRUCTIONS*

Follow the basic instructions. To create the handle, use approximately 36cm (14in) of plait (with a bushy tail at both ends), place it inside the item, and then secure one continuous handle around the length of the outside (approximately 67cm/27in). To secure the outside handle, simply sew through the holder, starting and finishing on the base of the item.

## Single Vase

The amount of raffia you need to complete a vase will obviously vary according to the size of the container you use as your mould. The following is provided as a guide.

*EQUIPMENT*

(For a vase 23.5cm (9in) high.)

◆ approximately 100g (3oz) raffia
◆ mould (try a variety of sauce or jam jars)
◆ sellotape
◆ needle

A single vase.

Opposite page: Larger containers, all still with inners so they remain waterproof.

Left: Shaker-style candle holder.

Above: The bottom of some vases, showing that not all are covered completely with raffia.

Above right: A nest of vases.

If you want to create a vase, you obviously need to incorporate a waterproof lining, and the jar you use as a mould can provide the perfect solution. To make sure the base remains secure, and the vase does not topple, do not cover the base of the jar; simply create a raffia skin.

*INSTRUCTIONS*

Start with step 1 of the basic instructions. Do not, however, cover the base of the mould. Instead, place the start of the plait around the base of the mould (in effect, creating the first row), and sellotape the bushy tail and sections of the row to the jar. Sew around the sides to the top of the mould – this leaves the base of the vase as flat (and secure) as the original jar.

When leaving the jar inside the raffia 'sleeve', you may also find it easier to finish the bushy tail on the outside as you will want it to be as tight to the jar as possible. If not, simply manoeuvre the sleeve to secure the bushy tail inside.

**USEFUL TIP:**

Creating this vase 'sleeve' gives your vase a secure bottom, but you can also gently lift it off if you want to clean the vase without getting the raffia soaked (although this would not damage it).

## Nest of Vases

*EQUIPMENT*

(As a guide.)

- total weight, including jars, approximately 1kg (2lb)
- moulds (3 jars of assorted height)
- sellotape
- needle
- glue gun

*INSTRUCTIONS*

Follow the instructions for creating the single vase (page 69), keeping the base of the jars uncovered. Once all the raffia sleeves are complete, position the vases in your chosen arrangement and glue horizontally together. Make sure you use enough glue to make a strong connection.

## Pots for Pens, Plants and Pot Pourri

If you discover a good mould (I found an old plastic tea, coffee and sugar set in Oxfam) you can easily give it a new lease of life. Here, I used the same set of containers to make different plant pots, but also kept one mould spare to make an assortment of containers.

## LIDS

Lids for your pots are an optional extra you might want to consider. You can choose from two versions.

### The Two-Piece Lid

This lid is made in two sections. Create a flat shape slightly larger than the top of the pot. Sew, and secure the finished bushy tail. For a circular pot you should end up with a small 'mat'. Take another

length of plait and sew it to the edge of the mat, completely round, until you have created the required depth of lid. This option gives a much flatter lid, with a more defined edge.

### The One-Piece Lid

Keeping your pot on the mould, start to sew a plait around the base as if starting again. It is important to keep the pot on the mould, as you need to ensure the lid will fit over the mould and the pot – it needs to be bigger than the pot itself. Continue to sew around the pot until you have sewn nearly to the required depth. Remove the lid from the mould and neatly finish the bushy tail. This lid option gives a more domed effect.

## LAMPSHADES

Using raffia is a great way to put new life into old lampshades, or to create an accessory that is completely individual to match a colour or design theme. I have described three methods, but you should always feel free to experiment.

Although the lampshades here are all circular in shape, this is no more

Far left: A range of containers from one mould shape (see back right).

Below left: Two-piece lid (left) and one-piece lid (right).

Below: the horizontal plait method (left) and the vertical plait method (right).

than coincidence, based on the mixture of frames with battered shades in my loft! These methods should work equally well on square or hexagonal frames – they might even prove to be easier to do, as they offer more places to hold the plait secure and therefore keep the lampshade the required shape (see this page, for the vertical plait method).

## Horizontal Plait Method

Using a circular frame 23cm (9in) high, with a top opening of about 45cm, and a base opening of about 126cm (50in), the final weight (including frame and raffia), is approximately 300g (10oz).

1.    Using the final weight provided as a guide, plait and trim approximately three-quarters of your raffia using the basic technique (five threads per knot and a four-knot plait). Create a bushy tail.

2.    Starting at the base opening, place the bushy tail inside the frame. Sew around, keeping your stitches secured around the frame.

3.    Once you are back level with the start bushy tail, push the plait to the outside of the frame and sew around the base again – this time sew not only around the frame, but also through the first row already in place.

### Note:
This method helps to secure the plait completely around the frame, and also means that the base of the frame cannot be seen.

4.    Continue sewing around the frame, making sure to sew a couple of stitches around the upright wires of the frame.

### Note:
The trickiest part of this lampshade is to make sure that, as you sew around, in the sections between the upright wires, you do not allow the shape to become too 'lax'. Try to keep it tight to the line of the final shape of the frame, otherwise it will start to look lumpy.

5.    Once you get to the top opening, sew around once on the outside so that the wire is completely hidden, and then sew the final row on the inside of the frame, so that the bushy tail can be secured out of sight.

## Vertical Plait Method

Using a circular frame 22cm (8in) high, with a top opening of about 43cm (17in), and a base opening of about 81cm (32in), the final weight (including frame and raffia), is approximately 250g (8oz).

1.    Using the final weight provided as a guide, plait and trim approximately three-quarters of your raffia using the basic technique (five threads per knot and a four-knot plait). Create a bushy tail.

2.    With approximately 2cm (just under an inch) on the inside of the frame, place the bushy tail over the top opening of the frame, directly over one of the 'upright' supports (one of the wires going from the top to the bottom openings).

3.    Sew through the bushy tail, 'astride' the upright, and then secure the plait all the way down the frame, making sure your stitches secure the plait to the upright.

4.    At the bottom of the frame, turn the plait inside, secure as for the top of the frame, and leave a length of

approximately 2cm (just under an inch) before finishing with another bushy tail.

5. Repeat from steps 2 to 4, until all the uprights of the frame are covered with plait.

6. Working between the uprights (which are now covered), place lengths of plait over the top, secure and sew to the lengths already in place on the frame, until the top opening has become fully covered.

**Note:**
There may be a considerable number of gaps around the frame.

7. To fill the gaps that are left (but do not go the full height of the frame), place lengths of plait inside to the beginning of a gap, and sew the sides of the plait to pieces already secured to the top and

Left: Examples of lampshades.

base of the frame. As the gaps get smaller, these pieces of plait will become shorter. Continue this until all the gaps have been covered by plait.

**Note:**
It is not necessary for these 'gap-fillers' to be secured over the top of the frame, but you should be able to secure the bushy tail over the base opening.

**Note:**
As a guide, the green lampshade in the photograph above, made using this method, has twenty-seven bushy tails secured over the top and forty-four bushy tails over the base.

### Twist and Tie Method

There is no plaiting involved with this method.

Using a circular frame 13cm (5in) high, with a top opening of about 26cm (10in), and a base opening of about 42cm (17in), the final weight

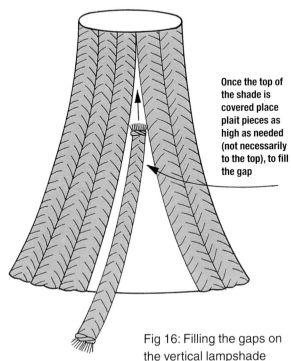

Once the top of the shade is covered place plait pieces as high as needed (not necessarily to the top), to fill the gap

Fig 16: Filling the gaps on the vertical lampshade

(including frame and raffia) is 125g (4oz).

1. With this method take time to cover all parts of the frame with raffia. Take a healthy raffia thread and coil it around all the wires of frame until the wires are completely covered.

2. Take three raffia threads and tie a knot part way along their length. Take these threads and coil around the top and bottom of the frame to cover the frame.

3. Once the threads are getting short, secure new threads (with a knot if preferred), to continue the same pattern.

4. To hold the threads in place, stitch around the top and bottom of the frame with a basic stitch.

## Note:

The knot effect does not add anything except extra detail. The pattern would work just as well simply twisted over the top and bottom of the frame.

## FLOOR MAT

The cost and durability of raffia mean that it is an ideal material for matting. It is the perfect choice to brighten up a kitchen or conservatory, although I recommend fixing non-slip matting to the reverse of your mat if you intend to use it on a polished or tiled floor.

*EQUIPMENT*

(For an oval mat 77cm (31in) by 52cm (21in) (as a guide).)

- approximately 400g (14oz) raffia
- needle
- non-slip matting (optional)

*INSTRUCTIONS*

1. Knot, plait and trim approximately three-quarters of your raffia as for the five-thread, four-knot plait. Create a bushy tail at the start of your plait.

2. As you are creating the mat without any need for a mould, you are completely free to choose the shape of your mat. The best options (for a more regular finish) are circular or oval. Simply make your first bushy tail turn to reflect the desired finished shape, and carry on sewing to the required size.

3. To finish, start to fade away your plait so that it is secured on the underneath of the mat by the time you come level with your bushy tail. Make sure you keep your outside edge as even as possible, by fading your plait carefully on the underneath of the mat.

## PICTURE FRAMES

Using raffia is a wonderful way of livening up an old or battered picture frame. The amounts of raffia needed obviously depends on the size of frame used. The general equipment needed is the same for each method, and amounts are included as a guideline.

Right: Two picture frame options.

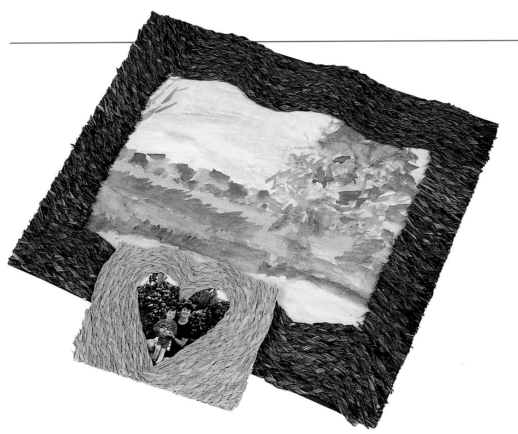

### EQUIPMENT

- ◆ picture frame or glass clip frame
- ◆ glue gun
- ◆ for glass clip frame 21 x 15cm (8 x 6in), using two threads per knot (see smaller photograph above), the total weight (including frame) is 300g (10oz)
- ◆ for glass clip frame 50 x 40cm (20 x 16in), using two threads per knot (see main photograph above), the total weight (including frame) is 1.7kg (3lb)
- ◆ for picture frame 23.5 x 21cm (9 x 8in), using four threads per knot (see photograph on opposite page, smaller frame), the total weight (including frame) is 300g (10oz)
- ◆ for picture frame 33.5 x 28.5cm (13 x 11in) using four threads per knot (see photograph on opposite page, larger frame), the total weight (including frame) is 1kg (2lb)

A glue gun is essential for picture framing with raffia. It makes the project very quick, and also gives a very secure fixing. Be warned, however – the plait is quite porous when hot glue is fixed to the frame, and you need to be careful of your fingertips!

The method for creating raffia picture frames is the same throughout – copious amounts of glue and the raffia plait secured in place (see photographs opposite and above), for a few ideas. It is important not to trim the plait until you have glued it; this ensures that you have enough plait to cover the area you need to cover. Also, the raffia is not easy to unpick from the frames once the glue has set.

The easiest frames to work with are the glass clip frames. I have not tried perspex, as it might be intolerant of the hot glue. As you can see in the photograph above, the fact that the surface is completely flat and clean means that you can experiment with the final shape you want. I have used two-thread knot plait on the clip frames, but this is not essential.

Above: Two clip-frame options.

# 10 Table Accessories

The durability of raffia means that you can create a range of accessories that can withstand heat, spills, and general wear and tear. These accessories can be created in colours, sizes and styles to suit your table.

## TABLE MATS

I have developed two basic techniques for table mats, both of which are equally versatile and attractive.

## Big Plait Method

*EQUIPMENT*

- approximately 50g (1oz) raffia for six coasters (10cm/4in in diameter)
- approximately 200g (7oz) raffia for six dinner mats (20cm/8in in diameter)
- approximately 200g (7oz) raffia for one large (40cm/16in in diameter)
- needle

*INSTRUCTIONS*

1.  Plait approximately three-quarters of your raffia using the basic technique (five threads per knot and a four-knot plait). Create your bushy tail.

2.  Thread your needle on the long thread left hanging from the bushy tail.

3.  As you are making a circular mat, you will need to make the first turn of the plait very sharp. With the granny knot pointing away from you, simply turn the bushy tail sharply back on itself to the right (left). Do not create an oval loop.

4.  Continue sewing through the flesh of the plait in a circular shape until you have nearly reached the required size.

5.  To finish each mat you need to taper the plait behind the previous row (on the bushy tail side of the mat), so that the outside edge of the mat is a smooth circular finish.

6.  Once you have created the final shape and sewn the plait past the bushy tail, sew up and down in a straight line on the plait to secure the width. Create the final bushy tail using a new thread to tie a tight knot with the last of your sewing thread.

7.  Ironing of these mats is optional and depends very much on whether you want a more finished or rugged look to the mats.

## Small Plait Method

The look of these mats is quite different from that of the big plait mats, and they take considerably longer to make. The biggest difference is that, although you do a four-strand plait, you only use two threads per strand. This is what takes the time.

Opposite: A range of table mats, with napkin rings. On the left, mats and coaster made using the big plait method; on the right, the same, made using the small plait method.

**USEFUL TIP:**
You might find it easier to use a circular needle to pick up part of the plait as you move round the shape. As the final result of this plait is very dense, it is not necessary to sew through every part of the plait as you go round.

*EQUIPMENT*

◆ approximately 180g (6oz) raffia for six coasters (10cm/4in in diameter)
◆ approximately 600g (21oz) raffia for six dinner mats (20cm/8in in diameter)
◆ approximately 300g (10oz) raffia for one large (40cm/16in in diameter)
◆ curved needle

*INSTRUCTIONS*

1.    Plait approximately three-quarters of the raffia using the basic four knots technique, but only using two threads per knot. Create your bushy tail.

2.    Thread your needle on the long thread left hanging from the bushy tail.

## Note:

The difference in sewing this mat is that, instead of sewing edge to edge as for other items, you are going to sew with the plait width to width. In effect, the edges of the plait will come in contact with the table, not the width of the plait, as with other mats.

Fig 17: Small plait method, width to width

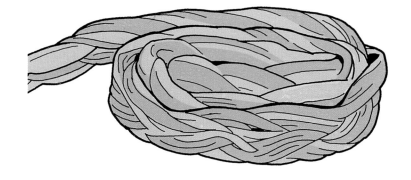

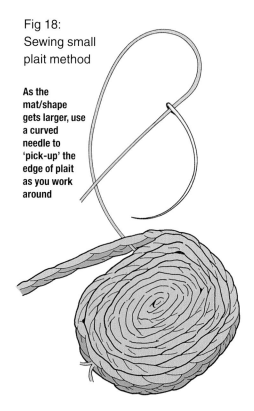

Fig 18:
Sewing small
plait method

**As the mat/shape gets larger, use a curved needle to 'pick-up' the edge of plait as you work around**

3.    Turn the bushy tail immediately back on itself (approximately 2cm, or less than an inch), and sew through both pieces of the plait.

4.    Continue sewing in a circular shape, with the plait width to width.

5.    To finish each mat, simply find a suitable place to stop and secure the end of the plait with a finishing bushy tail.

## Note:

I would not recommend pressing these mats, as this would flatten the upright effect of the plait, which is its appeal.

## Mat Shapes

This is an extension of the basic small plait method.

*EQUIPMENT*

- raffia – the amount will depend on the size of the item; refer to the dimensions of the small plait method
- outline of the shape to be reproduced
- piece of wood or cork
- tacks and hammer
- pegs (optional)
- needle and raffia for sewing, or
- hot-glue gun

*INSTRUCTIONS*

1.	Follow step 1 of the instructions for the small plait method.

2.	Place the outline shape on the piece of wood or cork and nail tacks in place along the edge of the shape at intervals of approximately 2.5cm (1in).

## Note:
Be sure to secure tacks to any 'extreme' parts of the shape where the plait will need to make an exaggerated turn.

3.	Place the start of the plait upright (as for the small plait method) around

Fig 19: Creating mat shapes

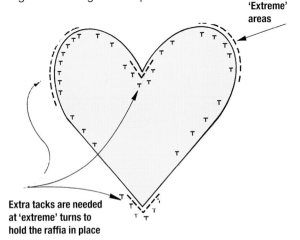

'Extreme' areas

Extra tacks are needed at 'extreme' turns to hold the raffia in place

**USEFUL TIP:**

If you are sewing, as the item gets larger you will find it difficult to sew through all the rows to the outside edge. Simply sew through enough of the adding row and existing rows to secure the new plait.

the outside of the tacks. At the starting point, leave the start bushy tail on the outside of the shape.

4.	Working to fill the inside of the shape (and the tacks), go round placing the plait width to width to the plait already placed outside the tacks.

5.	From this point, adopt one of two methods – either sew or glue the plait in place.

6.	To sew – as you work around the inside of the shape, either sew through the width of both the outside and the new inside row, or use pegs to secure a small area to return and sew.

7.	To glue – as you start to place new plait around the inside of the shape, drop a small amount of glue between the outside and inside rows to hold them together, being careful not to glue the plait to the tacks.

## Note:
If you are not used to working with a glue gun, remember, they are very effective and quick, the glue gets extremely hot, and, because the plait is porous, you need to be very careful.

8.	Whether sewing or glueing, continue working to fill the inside of the shape until you have filled approximately

**USEFUL TIP:**

If your shape has particularly exaggerated inward-pointing edges when you are nearing the end of the mat, you can sew a few stitches, pulling this part towards the centre of the shape, to accentuate the shape.

one-third of it. If it is difficult to continue sewing while the shape is nailed to the wood or cork, remove it and continue to fill the middle.

## NAPKIN RINGS

If you have created a set of table mats, you might like to extend your range to napkin rings. These are simple, and use very little raffia.

*EQUIPMENT*

◆ approximately 60g (2oz) raffia for six small rings

### Single Circle

Take a length of plait (four-knot, five threads per knot method) approximately 25cm (10in) long. Create a bushy tail at either end, leave one of the tails with a long tail, approximately 4cm (1in), and keep the other short. Curl the plait so that the short tail can be sewn and hidden underneath the long tail. This method leaves you with one long tail extending from the ring.

### Double Circle

This is an extension of the single circle style. Take a length of plait (four-knot method, five threads per knot) approximately 45cm (18in) long. Create a bushy tail at either end, with approximately 4cm (1in) of tail left extended. Curl the plait and sew it edge to edge, so that the final result has the long tails pointing in opposite directions. You can choose not to disguise the bushy tail finishes, but simply leave them pointing 'wild' from either side.

### Hidden Tails Method

If you prefer a less wild look, use this method. Take a piece of plait approximately 50cm (20in) long (five threads, four-knot method), and create short bushy tails at either end. Find the centre point and cut the plait, and secure the cut ends with short bushy tails. Curl the pieces of plait and hide the bushy tail at one end behind the opposite tail. For a wider napkin ring, sew the two rings edge to edge. Finally, you will need to hide the bushy tails that are now visible on the outside of the ring. You might do this with a shell or perhaps a raffia daisy.

Below: Napkin rings.

## SERVING-DISH BASKETS

This simple idea helps to keep your table co-ordinated, and makes an attractive finish for plain or ornate dishes. The amount of raffia required will depend on the size of the dish.

### EQUIPMENT

◆ for an oval dish 20cm x 13cm x 5cm (8 x 5 x 2in), approximately 100g (3 oz) raffia
◆ for a circular dish 14cm (5in) diameter, 4cm (1in) in depth, approximately 50g (1oz) raffia
◆ needle
◆ sellotape

*INSTRUCTIONS*

The method is exactly the same for both sizes of basket. Plait and trim the raffia (using the five-thread knot method), and keep a few strands aside for sewing (you do not need much on so small an item). Create your bushy tail and make the first turn to correspond with the shape of the item to be covered. Once you have sewn to the size of the base of the item, secure to the dish and continue to sew around the dish to the correct depth. To finish the item, you need to remove the raffia from the dish and hide the bushy tail neatly inside the basket.

Above: Serving-dish baskets.

# 11 Finishing Touches

This is where you can really give full rein to your artistic flair. The sky's the limit with the trims or finishing touches that you can put on hats, bags and other projects. The creation of finishing touches leads to the individual, one-off creations that make craft work rewarding.

I tend to be conservative with decorations, with a view to what will appeal to my customers, but I do enjoy seeing the variations that students and customers themselves bring to their hats and bags. Some of the finishes described here were produced by students and tailored by me.

As raffia is a natural material, I like to keep my decorations natural-looking, disliking any effect that is too synthetic. Artificial flowers can give too much of a contrast with the general look of the hat. Take advantage of the versatility of raffia, and you will not need to use synthetic materials. I choose raffia as a decoration over any other material.

I recommend that you make your finishing touches detachable as far as possible, particularly on hats, so you can ring the changes when you feel like it.

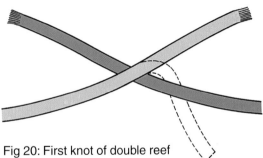

Fig 20: First knot of double reef

## RAFFIA TWIST AND KNOT

(With thanks to Crondall, February 1998 class for their help.) This is a double reef knot with a twist, and is one of the most popular finishes I use on my hats. It is a simple way to provide an attractive trim and can be very easily removed.

1.    Take twenty to thirty raffia threads, and make sure there are no unusual 'kinks' in them. Twist the threads together a little to tidy them up.

2.    Place a hat on your knee with the bushy tail finish towards your body. If you have made a Breton style, make sure the brim is down, as it will be easier to manage.

3.    Put the raffia twist around the hat and make sure the ends left to tie the knot are of equal length.

4.    Take the left side over the right and take it under the same piece towards the top of the crown.

5.    Keep an over-hand (knuckles uppermost) hold on the (new) right-hand piece and on the left-hand piece.

6.    Lift and turn the hat so that the front of the hat is now closest to your body. Complete the second knot in this position by taking the right hand over and through the gap now created by the left-hand position. Pull the ends tightly to secure the knot.

Opposite page: Single vase with a raffia twist.

**USEFUL TIP:**
This knot can work itself a little loose, so ease it a little, put an all-purpose glue inside, and then re-tighten.

## Note:
There is a knack to getting a good double reef for a hat trim. If you find that your knots end up with one tail pointing skywards, you have missed out the hat turn at step 6. Simply untie the twist and repeat.

7. Before you trim your knot ends, always make sure that your knot is in line with the bushy tail inside the crown of the hat.

## EMBROIDERY
Even if you are not very good at producing beautifully neat stitches, do not be put off from experimenting with embroidery on your raffia projects. If your embroidery lacks impact and precision, make up for it in enthusiasm!

Below are a few basic ideas and stitches to get you started. Before you start, sketch the ideas in rough, preferably in pen on the raffia, or sew a draft outline. Simply unpick the outline once you have finished.

## French Knots
Cut a raffia thread that is approximately one and a half times the length of your needle. From the inside of the item bring the needle through where you want it to be, keeping a hold on the thread as it comes through. With the needle only just above the item, twist it around the raffia two or three times. Keep the raffia taut around the needle so that the loops stay tight, and push it down immediately next to where you came through from the inside. Gently secure the two ends on the inside of the item — if you try to secure them too forcefully, you will pull the stitch apart.

## Lazy Daisy Stitch

From the inside of the item, bring the needle up at place A and down at B. Do not pull all the raffia thread through the plait. Take the needle through at place C, with the raffia under the needle, pulling gently to form the loop of the daisy. In one movement, make the final insertion at D back to A.

Right: French knots and a raffia twist as a finish on a Breton hat.

Below: Enthusiastic embroidery.

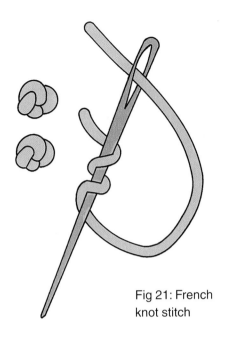

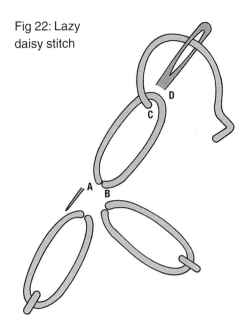

Fig 22: Lazy daisy stitch

Fig 21: French knot stitch

## Romanian Stitch

This stitch is good if you are looking for a block of colour on an item. Decide on the shape of the area you want to fill, then work from the top downwards. Bring the raffia thread through at point A, and back in at point B, keeping the thread below the needle, and coming out at C. Make a small diagonal stitch over the sewn thread to point D, and emerge on the direct left side of initial point A. Continue filling the shape in this manner.

## Coral Stitch

This stitch gives a nice line effect but can also be used to provide a block detail. Bring the raffia thread through from inside at A. Keep the thread down along the line you want to take and put the needle through just above the raffia at point B. Put in a small slanting stitch to just under the sewn line at C. Pull through the raffia loop to make the knot. Repeat this sequence for the shape or line needed.

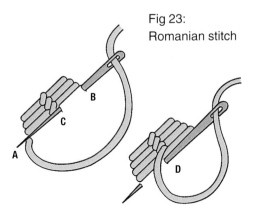

Fig 23: Romanian stitch

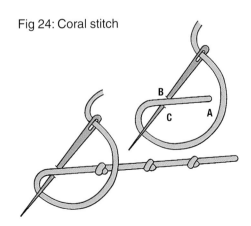

Fig 24: Coral stitch

**USEFUL TIP:**
If you are looking for a 'fuller' daisy, go around more than twice.

Fig 25: Starting a daisy

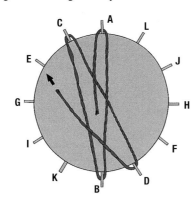

Fig 26: Beginning the daisy centre

Fig 27: Final daisy stages

**USEFUL TIP:**
Keep the excess thread on the needle, and use it to attach the daisy to the finished item.

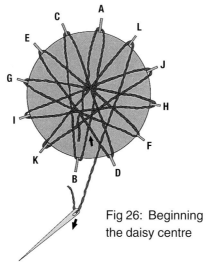

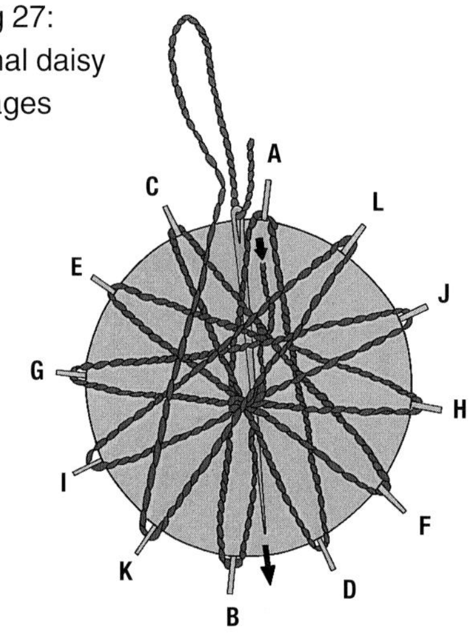

# DAISIES

Although metal spring-loaded daisy wheels provide an ideal size for daisies for hats, bags and hairclips, larger plastic daisy shapes are available from general craft shops, and these make useful daisies for larger objects. As with many projects, it is important that you use good-quality, long raffia.

*INSTRUCTIONS*

1. Place the end of one long strand of raffia in the centre of your daisy wheel and hold with your left (right) thumb. With your right (left) hand, twist raffia around A and then down around B. Go around A and B a second time before twisting the raffia around C and D.

2. After you have completed A and B, C and D, E and F, G and H, start another long strand of raffia and continue twisting around each spike and its opposite until you are back at the beginning, at A.

## Note:

Avoid the temptation to work to the very end of the first strand. This will probably be messy, and you will need to start a new strand to make sure you have enough to sew with.

3. When you have completed the circle, thread your needle with the remaining raffia that is attached to the daisy wheel.

## Note:

I recommend a longer and thicker darner than normal for this, as it will need to be forced underneath a concentrated amount of raffia.

4. Feed your needle under the raffia in the centre of the daisy, between A and

L, and out between K and B. Repeat this (under C and A, and out between B and D) around the wheel securing each section.

5. If you are using a spring-loaded daisy wheel, turn the knob and remove the wheel. If you are using a larger plastic daisy, simply lift the daisy off.

6. To secure your sewing thread, feed your needle through the daisy centre.

You can either leave the petals of the daisy as a round, or you can fluff the daisy. To fluff it, take a sharp pair of scissors and cut at the extreme end of each petal. Gently rub the edges of the cut petals, all the way around the daisy, to spread the edges and create a different look.

## QUICK TASSELS

These are ideal for a number of unusual decorations, on hats, bags and

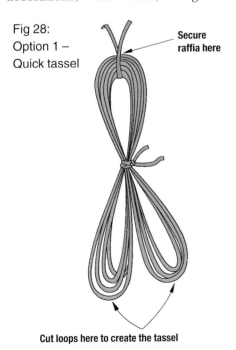

Fig 28:
Option 1 –
Quick tassel

**Secure raffia here**

**Cut loops here to create the tassel**

containers. Larger tassels can also be made, for holding back curtains. The technique for all quick tassels is exactly the same, but the more threads you use, the larger and more dramatic the effect.

For all the tassels described here, take approximately four healthy raffia threads.

## Method 1

Fold the raffia to a little more than twice the desired length of the tassel. Tie a piece of raffia around the top of the threads, pulling them together. Place another small piece of raffia around all the threads near the centre point to create the tassel effect. Cut the bottom loops to create the tassel (see Fig 28).

## Method 2

For a fuller or larger tassel, use a piece of stiff card that is just a little deeper than the desired length of the finished tassel. Place a single thread along the top edge of the card. Wind the raffia threads for the tassel around the card as many times as you want to get the fullness you need, making sure you can still see (and get hold of) the single horizontal thread. Pull this thread tightly to form the top of the tassel, and cut the raffia free from the card at the bottom edge. Finish the tassel off near the top with raffia around to pull it tight.

## QUICK BOWS

If you are not proficient at creating beautiful bows, here are two quick methods that provide a very nice finish, and appeal to my love of a simple, stitch-free approach. (See photo page 38.)

**USEFUL TIP:**
It is worth taking time to do this well, otherwise the result may be a crooked lining.

Opposite: Lining a hat with pins inside the crown as well as around the brim.

**USEFUL TIP:**
If you do not want to go to the trouble of fixing a whole lining, but find the front of the hat uncomfortable on your forehead, place a piece of sticky-backed towelling (as used on racket handles) just inside the front of the crown band.

Fig 29: Pinched bow

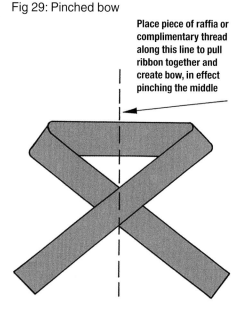

Place piece of raffia or complimentary thread along this line to pull ribbon together and create bow, in effect pinching the middle

## Pinched Bow

You will need approximately 50cm (20in) of ribbon, with the ends either neatly finished or with a 'V' cut out. Place the ribbon as in Fig 29. Take either a complementary thread, piece of raffia or ribbon, and place over the ribbon, following the dotted line indicated on Fig 29. Pull the thread tight around the ribbon to pinch it all together and form a bow. Secure it and then sew it to the item – in the example on page 38, I used raffia to fix the bow to the hat.

## Flat Bow

For this I used black cotton upholstery tape. To decorate a hat, you will need approximately 1m (3ft 3in) of ribbon. Starting at the back of the hat, place the ribbon around the crown band once. When the ribbon overlaps (at the back), either sew or glue it together. Working either from the left or right, move an equal distance in either direction, folding

the ribbon and returning to the centre. Repeat this until you have the desired number of 'pleats' in the bow (see Fig 30). Work until you have enough 'pleats' or until you have enough ribbon left to secure at the centre of the bow.

To finish, fold the end of the ribbon inside the final fold (as a tube). To secure, pin the bow in shape and remove from the hat in order to sew through all the layers of ribbon, and hold the bow in place.

## LINING A HAT

It is not essential to line hats, but some people do prefer the feel of a lining to the raffia.

Take a hat lining shape and pin it in place. The key to this is always to pin the 'extreme' of the hat – inside the deepest part of the crown. This ensure that, when the hat is worn, the head can still reach the whole crown. Once you have pinned the depth of the crown, work around the crown band and pin the lining in place.

Once you are happy with the positioning, use a complementary cotton thread to sew the lining to the crown band, and to put a few stitches where you have pinned inside the crown. This stops the lining being too loose.

Fig 30: Flat bow

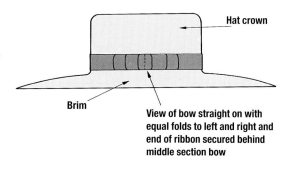

Hat crown

Brim

View of bow straight on with equal folds to left and right and end of ribbon secured behind middle section bow

# 12 Child's Play

Nothing in this book is exclusively an adult project. However, as a starting point for children, and for those who want to see quick results, the Alice band and hairclip projects provide a great introduction to raffia craft. Cheap to produce, these items are also wonderful for using up very small amounts of raffia, and for individual birthday or Christmas gifts.

One cautionary note: this chapter relies very heavily on my trusted glue gun – potentially an extremely dangerous tool in the wrong hands. Although the glue gun gives very quick and longer-lasting results, cold multi-purpose glue will work just as well in the short term, and will be safer for children to use, with supervision.

## ALICE BANDS

*EQUIPMENT*

- ◆ 'bare' Alice band (a plastic one from good craft shops, or an old band with the covering removed)
- ◆ raffia threads or plait to cover (depending on the width of the band, and on the decoration planned, sometimes as few as four threads)
- ◆ glue gun or cold adhesive

*INSTRUCTIONS*

Very simply, using either enough threads to cover the band, or raffia plait, glue the design to the band. For the purple band in the top photograph on the page opposite, I used two pieces of plait, and sewed them edge to edge before gluing them to the band. For the pink band with purple detail, the band was covered with a raffia thread before the detail was stuck in place – this helped to avoid any white plastic showing through on the top of the band. The green band is a narrow version of the purple.

## HAIRCLIPS

*EQUIPMENT*

- ◆ 'bare' hairclips, available from good craft or bead shops
- ◆ raffia daisies, threads or plait to cover
- ◆ buttons, shells or similar, for additional decoration
- ◆ glue gun or cold multi-purpose adhesive

*INSTRUCTIONS*

Once again, this is an extremely simple method. Simply cover the hairclip with the decoration you choose. Be careful, both with the hairclips and with the Alice bands, to ensure that you use ample adhesive, and that the 'mechanics' of the hairclip (the metal clip itself) are hidden by the decoration.

Opposite top: Examples of Alice bands, and the 'bare' plastic band before decorating.

Opposite bottom: Examples of hairclips, a daisy wheel, and uncovered clips.

# Bibliography

Bawden, Juliet, *The Hat Book, Creating Hats for Every Occasion* (Charles Letts & Co Ltd)

*Collins Complete Book of Needlecraft* (Collins)

de Wit, H.C.D., *Plants of the World* (The Higher Plants II)

Hora, Bayard, *The Oxford Encyclopaedia of Trees of the World*

Idiens, Dale, and Ponting, K.G., *Textiles of Africa* (The Pasold Research Fund Limited)

Lewis, Annabel, VV Rouleaux, *The Ultimate Ribbon Book* (Conran Octopus Limited)

Owen, Peter, *Knots* (The Apple Press)

Picton, John, and Mack, John, *African Textiles* (British Museum Publications)

Wadsworth, Annie, *Practical Raffia Work* (E.J. Arnold & Son Limited)

# Suppliers

Claire E. Richards
Supplier of raffia, polystyrene hat
blocks, daisy wheels
31 Le Patourel Close
Christchurch
Dorset BH23 3EE
England
Tel: 01202 470265
E-mail: raffia@dial.pipex.com
WWW: ds.dial.pipex.com/raffia

Hanson's (Discount) Fabrics
Supplier of raffia, polystyrene hat
blocks, lampshade frames
Station Road
Sturminster Newton
Dorset DT10 1BD
England
Tel: 01258 472698

K.R. Snoxell & Sons Limited
Supplier of hat linings
22 Clarendon Road
Luton LU2 7PQ
England
01582 724704

Dylon International Limited
Supplier of synthetic dyes
Worsley Bridge Road
Lower Sydenham
London SE26 5HD
England
0181 663 4801

# Index

**A**

Adding new knots  22
Adding new sewing threads  40
Alice Bands  91
Anatomy of a Hat  33
Attaché Bag  61

**B**

Bag Handles  57
Bag Reinforcements  58
Bag 'Skirt'  58
Beach Bag  55
Black raffia  14
Blend Method  19
Block Method  19
Blocks
  – bandaging  34
  – making  34
  – sizes  34
Boiling pot  14
Bucket Bag  61
Bushy Tail
  – creating  24

**C**

Changing hat styles  50
Containers  67
Circular Handbag  62
Continuing Method  31
Coral Stitch  85

**D**

Daisies  86
Dead End Method  30

Discarding rubbish  23
Dried Flower Basket  66
Drying raffia  15
Dye Margin  11
Dyes
  – natural  13
  – synthetic  13
Dyeing
  – methods  14
  – process  13

**E**

Embroidery  84

**F**

Five plait  20
Fixers  13
Floor Mat  74
French knots  84

**H**

Hairclips  91
Hat crown depth  39
Hat styles
  – basics  43
  – Breton  45
  – choosing  43
  – Cloche  49
  – Formal  47
  – Sewn-back Sun hat  49
  – Sun hat  44
Head
  – measuring  34
Horizontal Plait Lampshade  72

**I**

Introducing new colours 30
Ironing a hat 50

**L**

Lampshades 71
Lazy Daisy Stitch 84
Leather 18
Lining a hat 88
Log Basket 66

**M**

Materials 11

**N**

Napkin rings 80

**P**

Picture frames 74
Plait tension 17
Plaiting & other materials 17
Plaiting checklist 24
Plaiting more than
    one colour 18
Pot lids 71
Pots 67, 71
Pre-dye solutions 13

**R**

Raffia length 12
Raffia twist and knot 83
Rinsing 13

Romanian Stitch 85
Rubbish 12

**S**

Salt 13
Seagrass 18
Serving Dish Baskets 81
Sewing basics 27
Shaker-Style Candle Holder 69
Silky cotton 18
Sorting 11

**T**

Table Mats
    – big plait 77
    – shapes 78
    – small plait 77
Tassels 87
Trimming 23
Twelve plait 20
Twist & Tie Lampshade 73

**V**

Vases
    – nest 70
    – single 69
Vertical Plait
    Lampshade 72

**W**

Waste Paper Basket 66
Wool 18